# SIGNALS IN THE 1962 WAR

# SIGNALS IN THE 1962 WAR

Major General V.K. Singh

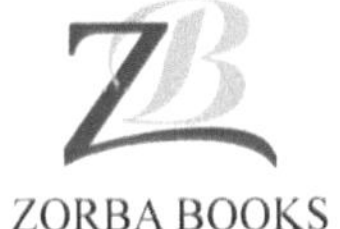

ZORBA BOOKS

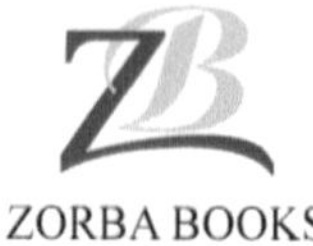

ZORBA BOOKS

Published by Zorba Books, January 2022

Website: www.zorbabooks.com
Email: info@zorbabooks.com



Title :- SIGNALS IN THE 1962 WAR

Printbook ISBN :- 978-93-93029-41-6
Ebook ISBN :- 978-93-93029-42-3



**Zorba Books Pvt. Ltd. (opc)**
Sushant Arcade,
Next to Courtyard Marriot,
Sushant Lok 1, Gurgaon – 122009, India

**Cover Photo:** (Left to right)
Captain Lakshman Singh,
Lieutenant Colonel K.K. Tewari,
Major Ram Singh

# DEDICATION

During the 1962 war, 51 signallers were killed in action. During the 1965 war, the number of signallers killed was 41, while in the 1971 war it was 33. Considering that in 1962 only one infantry division took part in the operations in NEFA and one infantry brigade in Ladakh, the casualties suffered by Signals were substantial. This book is dedicated to the following signallers who were killed in action during the Indo-China war in 1962:-

| Army No | Rank | Name | Date of Casualty |
|---|---|---|---|
| IC-6366 | Major | Ram Singh | 20 Oct 1962 |
| 6273649 | Signalman | A. Rahim Khan | 20 Oct 1962 |
| 6275568 | Signalman | Ram Dhan | 20 Oct 1962 |
| 6256568 | Lance/Naik | C.A. Chandy | 20 Oct 1962 |
| 6272031 | Signalman | R. Dayananda Prakash | 20 Oct 1962 |
| 6278044 | Signalman | M.D. Salamuddin K. | 20 Oct 1962 |
| 6269150 | Signalman | Atiwal Singh | 20 Oct 1962 |
| 6240845 | Lance/Naik | N. Siva Dass | 21 Oct 1962 |
| 6268368 | Signalman | Ram Singh | 21 Oct 1962 |
| 6279151 | Washerman | C. Kannan | 21 Oct 1962 |
| 6276060 | Signalman | Rathnam V. | 21 Oct 1962 |
| 6274938 | Naik | K. Nallaiah | 23 Oct 1962 |
| 6274701 | Signalman | Mohan Reddy | 27 Oct 1962 |
| 6265706 | Signalman | Chandra Sekhar Rai | 31 Oct 1962 |
| 6275696 | Signalman | Bihan Kumar Saha | 16 Nov 1962 |

| | | | |
|---|---|---|---|
| 6270981 | Signalman | Balwant Singh | 16 Nov 1962 |
| 6275184 | Signalman | Daya Sindhoo Prasad | 16 Nov 1962 |
| 6253914 | Lance/Naik | Sawinder Singh | 16 Nov 1962 |
| 6273177 | Signalman | Chaman Lal Sharma | 16 Nov 1962 |
| 6260741 | Signalman | R.K. Sarkar | 18 Nov 1962 |
| 6276589 | Signalman | M. Venu | 18 Nov 1962 |
| 6228622 | Havildar | Balwant Singh | 18 Nov 1962 |
| 6263758 | Signalman | Ram Raj Pandey | 18 Nov 1962 |
| 6267614 | Signalman | P.K. Sengupta | 18 Nov 1962 |
| 6273429 | Signalman | Rajpal Singh | 19 Nov 1962 |
| 6281937 | Signalman | Kulwant Singh | 19 Nov 1962 |
| 6244759 | Havildar | Bhagwan Dass | 19 Nov 1962 |
| IC-12546 | 2nd Lieutenant | D.K. Chopra | 19 Nov 1962 |
| 6267767 | Signalman | Sheik Mauhlla | 19 Nov 1962 |
| 6269336 | Signalman | K.C. Patnaik | 19 Nov 1962 |
| 6271899 | Signalman | Awtar Singh | 19 Nov 1962 |
| 6273402 | Signalman | Jeetmal Singh | 19 Nov 1962 |
| 6272772 | Signalman | S. Aseer Vadam | 19 Nov 1962 |
| 6242381 | Lance/Naik | T.K. Mohanan | 19 Nov 1962 |
| 6631727 | Signalman | S. Narayanan | 19 Nov 1962 |
| 6241973 | Lance/Naik | Abdul Gafoor | 19 Nov 1962 |
| 6235595 | Naik | Lalman Singh | 19 Nov 1962 |
| 6247935 | Lance/Naik | Chathunni | 19 Nov 1962 |
| 6269475 | Signalman | E.N. Karunakaran Nair | 19 Nov 1962 |
| 6276146 | Signalman | Anna Saheb Dhange | 19 Nov 1962 |
| 6250376 | Naik | Gurbaksh Singh | 19 Nov 1962 |
| 6262422 | Lance/Naik | Sher Singh | 19 Nov 1962 |
| 6271588 | Signalman | Hausala Prasad Tiwari | 19 Nov 1962 |
| 6279880 | Signalman | Sham Rao Naik | 19 Nov 1962 |
| 6280790 | Signalman | P.N.R. Nair | 19 Nov 1962 |
| 6268029 | Signalman | Swarn Singh | 19 Nov 1962 |
| 6278904 | Signalman | Munishwar Chand | 19 Nov 1962 |

| | | | |
|---|---|---|---|
| 6262106 | Signalman | Bichitra Singh | 19 Nov 1962 |
| 6277283 | Signalman | Mohan Singh | 19 Nov 1962 |
| 6277285 | Signalman | V.V. Nagarajan | 21 Nov 1962 |
| IC-8468 | Captain | K.S. Mann | 21 Nov 1962 |

# CONTENTS

# PREFACE

The coffee table book titled 'THROUGH – Saga of the Corps of Signals' was published in February 2001. I was then assigned the task of compiling the second volume of the history of the Corps of Signals of the Indian Army from the outbreak of World War II (1939) to Partition & Independence (1947). This book was published in February 2006, more than thirty years after publication of the first volume written by Brigadier Tery Barreto, which had been published in 1975. I was then assigned the task of compiling the third volume covering the first 25 years of the post- Independence history of the Corps of Signals, from 1947 to 1972. I began working on Volume III in 2007 and submitted the manuscript in 2010. A copy of the book was released during the Corps Centenary celebrations in Jabalpur in February 2011. After this, the project ran into rough weather due to problems concerning security clearance. Finally, after several deletions and changes, clearance was accorded in 2014 and the book saw the light of day in 2015.

According to the present policy on declassification of military records, all records from 1962 onwards are still classified. As a result, the entire chapter dealing with the 1962 war with China had to be deleted. It was intended to print it separately as a supplement, which can be added to the book at a future date, when records are declassified. Similarly, due to security considerations, some personal inputs from veterans who took part in the Nathula and Chola skirmishes in 1967 and the Indo-Pak war of 1971 in the Eastern Theatre were curtailed or omitted. Interestingly, the 'official' histories of 1962, 1965 and 1971 wars produced by the History Division of the Ministry of Defence are available on the website of Bharat Rakshak and can be downloaded. The histories of the 1962 and 1965 wars are graded 'Restricted' while that of 1971 does not bear any security classification. However, printed copies are not available.

Considering that only one infantry division was involved in the 1962 operations, the casualties suffered by Signals were substantial, and have not been matched in any subsequent operation. As one reads about the trials and tribulations that they suffered, one can only marvel at their fortitude and stupendous performance. It is a pity that the contribution of our brave predecessors is not known to the present generation of signallers. It is to fill this gap in our history that I decided to write this book. All references to military records such as war diaries have been omitted. The book is primarily based on books written by various authors, mentioned in the bibliography. In addition, personal inputs from officers who took part in the operations have been relied upon. Among them are Brigadier (late) K.S. Gill, Major General (late) K.K. Tewari, Brigadier Lakshman Singh, Brigadier Lal Singh, Brigadier (late) Tery Barreto, and several others. Some of them are no longer with us. I wish I had written this book ten years earlier, when most of them could have read about their achievements.

Gurgaon<br>December 2021

(V.K. Singh)<br>Major General

# Chapter 1

# INTRODUCTION

The Chinese invasion of India in 1962 took the country by surprise. It was the sequel of the failure of both countries to resolve the problems concerning the border between them. The political leadership, led by Nehru, believed that the Chinese would never attack India. This view was responsible for the 'Forward Policy', which envisaged the establishment of several posts along the border, which had never been delineated, to prevent Chinese incursions into Indian Territory. There were several minor incidents that should have given an indication of Chinese intentions, but these were ignored, due the prevailing belief that the China was not in a position to enter into a serious confrontation with India. The McMahon Line, which formed the basis of Indian claims, had never been accepted by the China. After the departure of Generals Thimayya and Thorat, the military was virtually side-lined, and their advice disregarded. V.K. Krishnamenon, B.N. Mullik and B.M Kaul became the Prime Minister's trusted advisers on all matters concerning the nations' security.

The Chinese invaded India according to a well prepared plan, with simultaneous attacks in NEFA and Ladakh. The first assault occurred on 10 October 1962 when the Chinese attacked and overran the Indian post at Tsenge Jong, which had been established on the north bank of the Namka Chu River. Ten days later they launched a massive attack in the Namka Chu sector as well as the Galwan valley in

Ladakh. After virtually destroying 7 Infantry Brigade that was holding the Namka Chu defences, they continued their onslaught, capturing Tawang. Further east the Chinese captured Kibithoo while in Ladakh they occupied Daulat Beg Oldi. There was a lull in the operations for about three weeks, during which both sides consolidated their positions and carried out preparations for further operations. Starting in mid-November 1962, the second phase in NEFA saw the fall of Walong, followed by Sela, Dirang Dzong and Bomdila in quick succession, most of the positions being vacated even before they were attacked. In Chushul in the north Rezangla and Gurung Hill fell after fierce fighting. On 21 November, the Chinese announced a ceasefire, ending hostilities on all fronts.

In NEFA, the major operations took place in the Kameng Frontier Division, where 4 Infantry Division was deployed. In the Lohit Frontier Division, an important battle was fought at Walong. The operations in these two divisions have been covered in detail. Some incidents also took place in the Subansiri and Siang divisions of NEFA, but these were minor in nature and have been omitted. Similarly, incidents on the Indo-Tibet border areas in Uttar Pradesh and Himachal Pradesh have been ignored, as there was little or no fighting. There were several actions in Ladakh, where the Indian troops fought gallantly, vacating their positions only after suffering heavy casualties or on orders from higher headquarters. These significant actions in Ladakh have been covered in fair amount of detail, the minor ones being omitted.

## Background

British and Chinese interests in Tibet came into conflict for the first time after Younghusband's expedition in 1903-4. Alarmed by the British Force, the Dalai Lama fled to China and the Regent *Tri Rimpoche* signed the Anglo-Tibetan convention, giving Britain trading and communication rights, along with the stationing of a British representative and military escorts in Tibet. During the subsequent Anglo-Chinese ratification of the convention in 1906, the British gave an assurance that they would not annex or interfere in the administration of Tibet, and the Manchu imperial government began to perceive Britain as a threat to its own suzerainty over Tibet. In 1910 a Chinese military force occupied Lhasa, forcing the Dalai Lama to flee again, this time to India. Recognising the growth of China's military power, Britain began to explore the extent of tribal territories in the region, in an attempt to establish control and forestall further Chinese excursions.

In 1911 the Manchu empire collapsed and the Dalai Lama returned to Lhasa. During a conference held at Simla in 1914, Sir Henry McMahon, the Foreign Secretary to the Government of India, prevailed on the Chinese and Tibetan representatives to accept the line drawn on a map indicating the limits of Inner and Outer Tibet. Though the Chinese representative reluctantly initialled the map, the government in Peking subsequently refused to ratify the agreement. Significantly, the Chinese objected to the alignment of the eastern boundaries of Tibet, not the alignment of the Indo-Tibet border, which ran along the crest line from the Bhutan border to the border of Burma with China's Yunnan province. To make the line straight and avoid a common border between Assam and Tibet, McMahon prevailed on the Tibetans to concede the Tawang salient to India. However, Tibet continued to administer Tawang and Dirang.

The proceedings of the Simla conference were never published, and the government of Assam remained unaware of the existence of the McMahon Line until 1935, when it was first marked on the maps of the Survey of India. In 1938 the Assam government sent a British officer with an escort which occupied Tawang and evicted the Tibetan officials. After vehement protests from Lhasa, the force was recalled and the Tibetan officials returned. However, Assam Rifles posts were established in Dirang and Walong. After India became independent in 1947, the situation remained unchanged for a few years, until China occupied Tibet. The Nehru government, without initiating negotiations with the Chinese, decided to extend its administration right up to the McMahon Line. In 1951 a political officer with a strong escort of Assam Rifles was sent to Tawang, evicting the Tibetan officials. The Chinese did not protest, leading the government in Delhi to assume their tacit acceptance of the McMahon Line. The next few years were the period of *Hindi Chini Bhai Bhai,* with Nehru and Chou En-lai professing everlasting friendship between the two Asian giants.

The reason for the Chinese silence became clear only later. Unknown to India, the Chinese had begun construction of a road across Aksai Chin in eastern Ladakh in 1951, soon after they occupied Tibet. The Chinese considered the road strategically important as it gave them easier access to western Tibet and Lhasa from Sinkiang via Aksai Chin, than over the Khampa dominated mountains of the east. India came to know of the road only in 1958 from a report of the Indian embassy in Peking. An Army patrol sent to the region was captured by the Chinese and released only after two months. Indian protests were summarily rejected by the Chinese, who blamed India for intruding into their territory.

Between August and October 1959 there were three serious border incidents which made the Indian public aware, for the first time, of the serious differences between China and India on the border issue. In August a party of 200 Chinese violated the border at Khinzemane in the Kameng Frontier Division of NEFA and pushed back the Indian patrol that met them. However, there was no clash and the Chinese later withdrew. Shortly afterwards another intrusion took place at Longju in the Subansiri Frontier Division, where the Chinese fired on an Indian post and apprehended the occupants. The Prime Minister informed Parliament about these incursions on 28 August 1959, adding that the government had decided to place the border areas in NEFA directly under the military authorities. Until then, the border posts were manned by the Assam Rifles, which functioned under the Ministry of External Affairs.

In September 1959 the Chinese laid formal claim to about 50,000 square miles of Indian territory in Ladakh and NEFA. The third major incident took place in October 1959, when the Chinese ambushed a police patrol party under Havildar Karam Singh in the Changchenmo valley, south of the Kongka Pass. Even as these border incidents were taking place, China had stepped up her repressive measures in Lhasa, culminating in the bombardment of the Norbu

Lingka summer palace in March 1959. Alarmed by this development, the Dalai Lama fled to India where he was given an enthusiastic welcome by the Indian people. The Chinese government accused the Nehru government of meddling in its internal affairs. This was the beginning of the cold war between India and China. The mask had fallen and the dispute between the two great powers of Asia was now out in the open.

Unfortunately, Nehru did not take these incidents seriously, taking the Chinese at their word that they would not resort to military force to resolve the border disputes. This was the view held by the Director of the Intelligence Bureau, B.N. Mullik, whose opinion Nehru trusted in these matters. The Army did not share this view, and General K.S. Thimayya, the Army Chief, as well as Lieutenant General S.P.P Thorat, the GOC-in-C Eastern Command, had informed the government in early 1959 of the Chinese threat and the men and material required to contain it. Both were dubbed 'alarmist' by the bureaucrats as well as the Defence Minister, V.K. Krishna Menon. The difference of opinion between them was one of the reasons for Thimayya's resignation on 31 August 1959 (which he later withdrew), and Thorat not being appointed the Army Chief after Thimayya's retirement in 1961. As was later learned, Krishna Menon did not inform Nehru about the paper prepared by Thorat and submitted to him by Thimayya in October 1959, which clearly brought out the serious shortcomings in the defence of NEFA in the event of a Chinese attack.

It would not be out of place to recount the incident regarding the paper submitted by General Thorat. After the Chinese over ran the defences in NEFA in 1962, there was a lull in the battle, which took place almost exactly as Thorat had predicted. Nehru sent for him and asked, "How could this have happened. You were in Eastern Command, did you have any inkling of this disaster?" Thorat replied "Yes Sir. The possibility had occurred to us and the Ministry was warned." When Thorat showed the paper he had sent in October 1959 to him, Nehru was stunned. "Why was this not shown to me," he asked. Thorat suggested that perhaps the Defence Minister could answer this question. At this Nehru exploded, "Menon, Menon! Why have you got your knife into him? You people do not realise what an intellectual giant he is."

Thorat said, "If he is, Sir, I have seen no evidence of it in the case under consideration." Nehru glared at him angrily, for a few seconds. Then he smiled, and said, "You know, Thorat, you Maharashtrians are like mules. Normally you are good and docile, but once you dig your toes in, it is impossible to dislodge you." The tension broke, and Nehru rang for some tea. He became once again the affable Nehru, who Thorat knew so well from the days of the Partition riots, and after his return from Korea. Nehru went on to discuss the possibility of the Chinese, who had declared a cease fire unilaterally, advancing into the Brahmaputra valley, Thorat told him that they were unlikely to do so, since their lines of communication were already stretched, and they could not get their artillery and tanks across the Himalayas. At this, Nehru perked up, and invited Thorat to be a member of the National Defence Council, which he was thinking of forming.

# Chapter 2

# EVENTS LEADING TO THE CONFLICT

## Operation 'Onkar'

The decision of the government to entrust the responsibility for guarding the northern border to the Army was taken in August 1959. However, due to logistical problems, it was only in November 1959 that 4 Infantry Division was ordered to move to Assam with its three brigades - 5, 7 and 11. The responsibility of 11 Infantry Brigade was to look after the 225-km long Sikkim-Tibet border. The other two brigades were to defend the 1075 km long NEFA-Tibet border i.e. the McMahon Line. The task of 7 Infantry Brigade was to guard the Kameng Frontier Division, while 11 Infantry Brigade was made responsible for the rest of NEFA. To improve the lines of communication in the border area, the General Reserve Engineering Force (GREF), also known as the Border Roads Organisation, was set up January 1960.

In 1960 Operation 'Onkar' was launched in NEFA. This envisaged the establishment of a large number of posts along the frontier, manned by Assam Rifles personnel under Army supervision. Strangely enough, the exact location was decided not by the Army but the Intelligence Bureau! In the Central Sector, i.e. the UP-Tibet border, due to administrative difficulties, Police Forces continued to be responsible for the defence of the border, though the Army commands were instructed to complete all preparations to enable regular troops to take over border security duties at short notice in an emergency. At this time, the UP-Tibet border was being guarded by six companies of Special Police Force (SPF). By July 1961 the strength of SPF had gone up to nine companies, seven of which manned 17 summer posts on the border, the rest being deployed in Jammu and Kashmir..

The decision to hand over the border in Ladakh was implemented in April 1960 with the induction of HQ 114 Infantry Brigade comprising 7 and 14 Jammu and Kashmir Militia battalions. In April 1961 the brigade was strengthened with the addition of 1/8 Gorkha Rifles and some ancillary troops. In spite of difficulties imposed by lack of road communications, shortage of aircraft, severe cold conditions and other logistical problems, the three battalions of the brigade were not only deployed in forward areas but a few additional posts were also established, bringing their number to 27 by the end of 1961. Of these, 11 were in the Nubra Valley Sector, six in the Chang Chenmo and Chushul Sector and ten in the Indus Valley Sector.

On 2 November 1961 an important meeting was held in New Delhi, during which the Prime Minister directed that Indian forces should occupy the whole frontier from NEFA to Ladakh and cover all gaps by setting up posts or by means of effective patrolling. However, he ordered that our troops should not fire except in self-defence. On 5 December 1961, Army HQ instructed Western Command to patrol as far forward as possible in Ladakh sector, with a view to establish additional posts to prevent the Chinese from advancing further and also to dominate existing Chinese posts. The order also specified that the 'forward policy' shall be carried out without getting involved in a clash with the Chinese unless it becomes necessary in self-defence. Regarding UP and other Northern areas similar instructions were issued, Eastern Command being told to go forward and occupy the whole frontier, covering the gaps by patrolling or by posts. As will be obvious, the orders from Army HQ went a step further than the instructions issued by the Prime Minister. The 'forward policy' was the genesis of the deterioration in the situation on the border, culminating in the Chinese attack and the final debacle. Though it has not been conclusively established who was responsible for the forward policy, it is generally believed that Lieutenant General B.M. Kaul, the Chief of General Staff and B.N. Mullik, the Director Intelligence Bureau, played an important role.

In spite of the difficult terrain, adverse weather conditions and lack of adequate maintenance facilities, a number of new posts were established near the McMahon Line and the strength of already existing posts was increased. Although those posts were being manned by Assam Rifles, they were physically established under supervision of the Army. The posts were in most cases of platoon strength and almost entirely dependent on air-dropped supplies. In February 1962 the Assam Rifles detachments had been posted at Chutangmu, Chuna, Khinzemane and Bum La in the Kameng Frontier Division. In Ladakh, by the time the implications of the new policy had been worked out, the winter of 1961-62 had far advanced. Hence it was only from April 1962 that the induction of troops commenced and a battalion was concentrated at Leh by mid-May 1962. Army units from Daulet Beg Oldi started moving eastwards and set up posts along the Chip Chap river valley, within a couple of kilometers of the Chinese posts. Although there were now four battalions posted in Ladakh, the force was inadequate to defend the 480 km front from Daulet Beg Oldi in the north to Demchok in the south. As a result, they had to be dispersed into small, isolated posts each barely 10 to 20 strong. This pattern of deployment was based on the known Chinese tactics, which was to creep into Indian Territory whenever it was unguarded, but not to launch an offensive against the Indian posts. By the end of September, 36 Indian posts had been established in Ladakh against 47 posts set-up by the Chinese in the region. Around Chushul the Indian and Chinese posts confronted each other at close range and in the south around Rezangla and Demchok the Indian posts reached almost up to the international border.

By May 1962 the Chinese had reinforced all their posts all along the Indo-Tibetan border. A report on the Frontier Security Situation prepared by the Intelligence Bureau was discussed on 17 May 1962 at a meeting presided over by the Defence Minister, who ordered that all the gaps left still unoccupied in the border areas should be filled up. Even if sizeable forces could not be spared, there should be at least a platoon of the Army or police or the Assam Rifles at each of those places. By 20 July 1962, 34 posts – 8 in Kameng, 8 in Subansiri, 7 in Siang and 11 in Lohit Frontier Divisions – had been established in NEFA. Among these posts was the one at Dhola, established a little south of the Namkha Chu on 4 June 1962 under the guidance of Captain Mahabir Prasad of 1 Sikh who accompanied the Assam Rifles party. In June 1962 HQ 4 Infantry Division designated Tawang as the Divisional Vital Ground. Consequently 7 Infantry Brigade was moved to Tawang to strengthen the defences of the town. The force level in NEFA at this time was two infantry brigades and 74 platoons of Assam Rifles.

Even as diplomatic efforts to resolve the dispute continued, the tension on the border increased as the Chinese inducted more troops in the region. By the beginning of September 1962 it was estimated that the total deployment of Chinese troops along the northern frontier had gone up by six battalions since the beginning of the summer of 1962. Of the total strength of Chinese troops in Tibet, which was of the order of eight divisions, almost seven divisions were dispersed in the south and south-western border areas. In addition two regiments (six battalions) were deployed opposite North Ladakh, almost double the force of three battalions that had been there in spring of 1962. In the area in front of South Ladakh and the central sector, the strength of Chinese troops had been increased from five to seven battalions. Against Sikkim, three regiments were deployed of which two were in the Chumbi valley and one opposite North Sikkim. Across NEFA, the estimated Chinese deployment was of the order of 19 battalions. In addition to the troops deployed on the border, three to four Chinese divisions were held as reserves in places like Lhasa, Gyantse, Shigatse, Chamdo and Nagchuka.

The above military preparations were followed by a spurt in provocative activities by Chinese troops and intrusions in Indian Territory. On 10 July 1962, about 300 Chinese soldiers surrounded the Indian post at Galwan manned by about 40 Gorkhas. The post was ordered to stand fast and did not withdraw, though the Chinese deliberately left a withdrawal route open. The Chinese did not permit the relief of the post and threatened to open fire on a party that was sent for the purpose in August. Consequently, the post had to be supplied by air. The post was subsequently overrun in October 1962 when the Chinese attack was launched.

Soon after the encirclement of the Galwan Valley incident, on 21 July 1962 a Chinese party opened fire with LMGs, mortars and rifles on a routine Indian patrol of 14 Jammu and Kashmir Militia, about eight km south-east of Daulet Beg Oldi. The patrol returned the fire in self-defence. In this action, one naik and one sepoy were seriously wounded. On the same day the Chinese fired on a patrol of 1/8 Gorkha Rifles, wounding two Indian soldiers. On 4 August 1962, the Chinese fired a shot near Karakoram Pass close to the Indian post at Daulet Beg Oldi. On 26 August at 12 pm, a party of the Chinese troops tried to ambush an Indian patrol on routine duty about 53 km south-east of Daulet Beg Oldi, but the attempt was detected and foiled. There was another incident of firing by the Chinese on an Indian patrol party in the Galwan Valley area on 2 September 1962.

In the Eastern sector, during the period June/July, the Chinese had intensified their border patrolling opposite the Subansiri and Siang Frontier Divisions. They had intruded about 140 metres inside Indian Territory at Lhola in the western part of Siang Frontier Division. Several senior Chinese officers were noticed carrying out reconnaissance in Subansiri and Siang Frontier Divisions. A Chinese VIP also visited the Thagla Ridge in July 1962. By that time, the Chinese had constructed a road up to Le village, approximately 10 km short of the McMahon Line. During the last few months, all Chinese border posts had moved forward and had been considerably reinforced. They had constructed defence works in all the forward posts and the troops had been issued modern machine-guns in place of the old weapons. Telephone lines had also been laid right up to the Frontier. The Chinese had deployed two companies opposite the Khinzemane Indian post and a company at Shao opposite Bumla. The biggest threat was posed by the Chinese in the Eastern sector in August when they moved troops to the Thagla Ridge in the Kameng Frontier Division and occupied it. By the end of August 1962, they had concentrated about 400 troops in the area.

## Operation 'Leghorn'

At this time HQ 7 Infantry Brigade under Brigadier J.P. Dalvi was located at Tawang, along with two battalions, 9 Punjab and 1 Sikh. On 23 August 1962, after a conference held at HQ 7 Infantry Brigade, 9 Punjab under Lieutenant Colonel R.N. Misra was ordered to move forward and occupy certain posts close to the border. Due to non-availability of adequate local ponies and porters, the move commenced only on 27 August and was in small parties. By 8 September 1962, one company had reached Shakti; one was at Lumpu, with the remainder still at Tawang. At about 3 pm the company at Shakti received a message that about 300-400 Chinese had crossed the Thagla Pass, demolished two bridges over the Namka Chu at 8 am and surrounded the Assam Rifles post at Dhola. By 4 pm the message had been passed on battalion wireless net to the Battalion HQ which immediately conveyed it to Brigade HQ on telephone.

The Dhola post had been established a month earlier as part of Operation 'Onkar'. It comprised 32 Assam Rifles personnel under a Junior Commissioned Officer. While setting up the post, the officer detailed for this task, Captain Mahabir Prasad of 1 Sikh, noticed that the traditional boundary was at variance with the boundary shown on the map. According to the map, Dhola post, which was situated near the tri-junction of Indo-Bhutan-Tibetan territory, fell north of the McMahon line, whereas traditionally the boundary ran along Thagla ridge which was to the north of the post. This had been confirmed from the local Political Officer and the Divisional Headquarters informed on 5 September 1962. In fact, the name Dhola post was a misnomer, as the actual name of the area, a small pasture on the south bank of Namka Chu River, was Tsedong. It came to be known as Dhola post after Dhola pass located about two miles to the south.

The post had been surrounded by the Chinese at 8 am but the information reached the Brigade Headquarters eight hours later at 4 pm. The inordinate delay in passage of such vital information needs scrutiny. The battalion apparently had only four 62 sets. One was with the Battalion HQ and one with the company at Shakti. The third set for the company at Lumpu was still on its way, while the fourth was with a platoon at Lumla. There was no direct communication with the Assam Rifles posts. As an ad hoc arrangement, the 62 set at Shakti tuned in to the Assam Rifles net twice a day at 9 am and 3 pm, and information obtained on this net was then passed on to the Battalion HQ on the battalion net. Communication between Battalion HQ and the company at Lumpu was through the Assam Rifles post at Lumpu, using the relay system. The system was unsatisfactory and caused a considerable amount of delay.

Commenting on the communications arrangements, Lieutenant Colonel (later Major General) K.K. Tewari, who was then commanding 4 Infantry Divisional Signal Regiment, said:

> *"Actually the problem was that Assam Rifles were to be passing the information. After all, all the border outposts were manned by the Assam Rifles. They would not give the information to the Army in the forward areas. They would pass the information to their own headquarters IGAR (Inspector General Assam Rifles) through their regimental headquarters. In the case of 5 Assam Rifles, which was manning the Kameng Division out post, their headquarters was at Lokra. The information took the route from Lokra to Shillong (HQ IGAR) and from there back to us (4 Divisional HQ)."*

Information of the Chinese move was conveyed to Divisional HQ and to Commander 7 Infantry Brigade, who had proceeded on leave, but was still at Tezpur. Orders were issued to the post commander at Dhola to hold out at all costs and reinforcements were on their way. Next morning the Brigade Commander arrived at Tawang by helicopter and conferred with Commanding Officers of 9 Punjab and 1 Sikh. He ordered 9 Punjab to move forward to Lumpu and 1

Sikh to send a company to Milaktongla. A strong patrol of 9 Punjab comprising 40 Other Ranks under Second Lieutenant N.C. Kohli was dispatched to the Namka Chu valley to find out the enemy strength and the extent of damage to the bridges. One Assam Rifles platoon ex Lumla was ordered to move forward to reinforce the Dhola post. Leave parties en-route to Misamari were stopped and were ordered to re-join their units. By the evening of 9 September the Chinese strength around Dhola was reported to be about 600.

During the next three days, several more patrols were sent out. After Kohli returned on 10 September and reported that there was no enemy at Bridge I, a patrol under a Junior Commissioned Officer was sent out to establish a firm base at that location. Two other patrols were sent to contact Dhola post, one along the Namka Chu River and the other via Karpola. None of these patrols had any means of communication. Leading a strong column of about three companies and two 3-inch mortars, the Commanding Officer, Lieutenant Colonel R.N. Misra, also reached Bridge I on the night of 14 September. Moving towards Bridge II next morning, he found the north bank occupied by Chinese, who began shouting at the Indians and asked them to go back as the area belonged to China. Leaving two companies at Bridge II Colonel Misra decided to make for Dhola. Since the north bank was occupied by the Chinese, his column moved south of the Namka Chu, reaching Dhola at 2 pm on 15 September. All this time there was no communication between the column and the base at Lumpu. It was only after reaching Dhola that Colonel Misra could convey the information to his Adjutant at Lumla, who in turn conveyed it to the Brigade Headquarters at Tawang. Instructions were received that the Indian Political Officer would be meeting his Chinese counterpart on 18 September, and nothing should be done to jeopardize the talks. After leaving a company at Dhola, Colonel Misra returned to Bridge II where the bulk of his unit was located.

Lieutenant Colonel K.K. Tewari, quoting from his diary, describes the above incident in the following words:

> *"On 14 September, we were all in the mess and this God Almighty flap was on when the IGAR came out with the dramatic news for the information of the Chief or the Corps Commander who was with us that day. .....I was talking about the IGAR breaking the news dramatically to steal the thunder, so to say, in the mess when he came and announced about the link up of the Army troops with Assam Rifles. The regular Army battalion, 9 Punjab, linked up with Assam Rifles at Dhola Post. This information had not been given to the Army in the forward areas. On this point I made a note in my diary and quote again: Signals getting blamed for 9 Punjab mistakes. Told GOC communications are OK but perhaps Assam Rifles and 9 Punjab are not on talking terms and Assam Rifles are deliberately withholding information".*

Along with the rapidly changing situation in the forward areas, considerable activity was taking place at higher echelons of the Army as well as the political leadership. On 9 September 1962, a high level meeting was held in Delhi, chaired by Defence Minister V.K. Krishna Menon. It was attended by the Chief of the Army Staff, General P.N. Thapar; GOC-in-C, Eastern Command, Lieutenant General L.P. Sen; the Cabinet Secretary, S.S. Khera; the Director, Intelligence Bureau, B.N. Mullik; and a few others. At the meeting it was decided that the Chinese must be evicted from south of the Thagla Ridge immediately. The Army Chief accepted the decision, and orders were passed to Eastern Command accordingly. To carry out this task, orders were issued for the immediate move of 9 Punjab to Namka Chu, with the rest of 7 Brigade to be ready to follow within 48 hours. The eviction operation was code-named 'Leghorn'.

Two days later at another meeting held in Defence Minister's office, General Sen reported that there were some 600 Chinese in Dhola and he had ordered 7 Brigade to deal with them. The estimate of Chinese troops was based on the wireless message received from the Junior Commissioned Officer at Dhola. Based on the advice of the Eastern Army Commander, the Defence Minister approved the decision to mount an attack on the Thagla ridge. On 12 September 1962, General Sen conveyed the decision of the government to expel the Chinese from Thagla to the Corps and Divisional Commanders during a conference at Tezpur. Lieutenant General Umrao Singh, GOC 33 Corps, who had already consulted the divisional and brigade commanders on the issue, clearly told the Army Commander that the task was beyond the capability of the troops available to him. He also questioned the wisdom of moving the only brigade available for the defence of Tawang, the vital ground, to Thagla. However, General Sen was not convinced, reiterating that the decision had been taken by the government, and they had to follow it. Immediately afterwards, General Umrao Singh sent a formal letter to Headquarters Eastern Command, giving a realistic appraisal of the military situation, based on an appreciation carried out earlier.

On 13 September, the Divisional Commander spoke to Commander 7 Infantry Brigade on wireless and ordered him to move to Lumpu forthwith. At the same time, 9 Punjab was ordered to move to Namka Chu. Brigadier Dalvi left Tawang next morning, accompanied by a staff officer and his rover group, reaching Lumla the same evening. After marching continuously for three days, he reached Lumpu on 16 September 1962. All this time, he was out of communication with his battalions as well as his staff. It was only after 16 September that HQ 7 Infantry Brigade became functional.

On 18 September, a Government spokesman announced at a press conference that the Army had been instructed to drive the Chinese out of the Dhola area. On 20 September, Eastern Command issued instructions that all patrols and posts were to engage Chinese patrols that came within range of their weapons. At this time, Brigadier Dalvi accompanied by Colonel Misra was carrying out reconnaissance of the area occupied by 9 Punjab. At 10.30 pm while they were at Bridge II discussing the points to be included in his appreciation that had been asked for by Divisional HQ, the Chinese sentry threw a grenade into the Indian sentry post. Firing started from both sides of the Namka Chu and resulted in two Chinese being killed and two wounded. Indian casualties were five wounded.

The outbreak of firing on the Namka Chu and the build-up by the Chinese made their intentions clear. At a meeting in the Defence Ministry on 22 September 1962, General Thapar asked the government to reconsider the decision to evict the Chinese from Thagla. Since Nehru and Krishna Menon were out of the country, the meeting was chaired by K. Raghuramaiah, the Deputy Defence Minister. The Foreign Secretary then explained the Prime Minister's instructions that no infringement of the border in NEFA was to be accepted. It was decided that the Army would have to carry out the instructions of the government and evict the Chinese from the Dhola area. General Thapar requested for a written order of the government on the subject. Soon afterwards, he received a note signed by H.C. Sarin, Joint Secretary, Ministry of Defence, which stated: *"The decision throughout has been as discussed at previous meetings, that the Army should prepare and throw the Chinese out as soon as possible. The COAS was accordingly directed to take action for the eviction of the Chinese in the KAMENG Frontier Division of NEFA as soon as he is ready."*

General Thapar repeated the Government's orders to Lieutenant General Sen. He also warned Lieutenant General Daulet Singh, GOC-in-C Western Command of the possibility of Chinese reaction in Ladakh and advised that Indian posts there should be strengthened. On 24 September the Corps Commander, Lieutenant General Umrao Singh personally conveyed these orders to Major General Niranjan Prasad, GOC 4 Infantry Division.

By this time, serious differences between commanders at various levels in the military hierarchy had surfaced. On 14 September, General Sen had ordered General Umrao Singh to carry out an appreciation and formulate an outline plan for the operation. After passing through the Corps and Divisional Commanders, the order reached Commander 7 Infantry Brigade. Other than the Army Commander, all three – Umrao, Prasad and Dalvi – were convinced that the capture of Thagla was not feasible with the resources then available. However, Dalvi agreed to produce an appreciation highlighting the maintenance and administrative problems, hoping that this would convince the higher authorities of the unsoundness of the plan. His appreciation resulted in a plan with the modest aim of capturing Tseng-jong, a small feature on Thagla slopes, and then rolling down west to east to the Chinese positions on the Namka Chu. It was to be attempted with an out-flanking move from Bridge V near Tsangle. While working out the logistics for the plan, Brig Dalvi made it clear that unless the proper administrative base was ready within a fortnight there would be no scope for operations during that winter.

The Divisional Commander approved the plan after some alternations and then submitted it to the Corps Commander who had reached Lumpu on 26 September. General Umrao Singh also suggested some modifications in the appreciation and advised on a more modest tactical aim. The draft plan was revised accordingly and the Corps Commander personally took it to Lucknow on 29 September. However, General Sen refused to accept the requirements stipulated for the operation; it would have been impossible to meet them before the winter set in. Being unable to convince the Army Commander, General Umrao Singh submitted his views and assessment of the situation in writing on 30 September. There were other differences between Generals Sen and Umrao, which came out in the open during a meeting on 2 October 1962, presided over by the Defence Minister. General Umrao protested at the interference in his command and orders sent to him by General Sen to send a company patrol to Tsangle to establish a post there. He felt that Tsangle had no tactical significance and would give away Indian intentions to the Chinese.

The Defence Minister returned from New York on 30 September. Two days later, Prime Minister Nehru returned from Nigeria. Sen had been insisting on the removal of Umrao and the appointment of a more pliable Corps Commander to carry out the orders of the government. The problem was solved by divesting General Umrao Singh of the responsibility for NEFA. It was taken away from XXXIII Corps and handed over to a newly raised IV Corps. Lieutenant General B.M. Kaul, the Chief of General Staff, was given command of the new Corps, with the specific task of evicting the Chinese from the Dhola-Thagla area.

Immediately after his appointment as Corps Commander, on 4 October 1962 Lieutenant General Kaul flew to Tezpur where, in an unprecedented reversal of protocol, he was received by the Army Commander himself. After spending the day in conference with Generals Sen and Umrao, he flew to Lumpu next day where he was received by the Brigade Major, the Commander having been sent forward the previous day by the Divisional Commander. Kaul promptly ordered HQ 7 Infantry Brigade to pack up and move to Tsangdhar immediately. Being out of touch with Brigadier Dalvi, the Brigade staff and Signal Company had little choice except complying with the order. Kaul then moved forward to Ziminthaung and Serkhim, where a helipad was constructed during the night on his orders. Accompanied by the Divisional Commander, he walked to Dhola on 7 October, where he was received by the Brigade Commander. Realising the enormous problems that the troops were facing, he sent a message to higher headquarters, informing them of these difficulties. Still he was all prepared to carry out the task assigned to him. In the plan that formed part of his appreciation, Brigadier Dalvi had specified 10 October as the date by which Op 'Leghorn' would have to commence if the required administrative and fire support was made available to him. Kaul decided to treat this date as a deadline, regardless of the rider about logistics.

On 7, 8 and 9 October General Kaul visited the posts and held discussions with their commanders. He took a number measures, such ordering 2 Rajput and 1/9 Gorkha Rifles to move from Tsangdhar to Namka Chu to join the other troops along the river line. Earlier, 9 Punjab had already been ordered to occupy Tsangle with one company. According to the plan which he disclosed to the subordinate commanders, in view of the difficulties of mounting a direct assault on Thagla he decided to make a "positional warfare" manoeuvre. Indian troops would occupy Yumtsola, to the west of Thagla peak which the Chinese had still not occupied. He hoped that this action would satisfy the government that the Army had done its best to carry out its orders.

Prasad and Dalvi tried to explain to Kaul that the troops in cotton uniforms would either freeze at Yumtsola or starve to death if their line of communication was cut off by the Chinese. Kaul brushed aside their objections. However, he agreed to Dalvi's suggestion to send a patrol from 9 Punjab before the whole battalion (2 Rajput) was committed. The patrol would find the best place to cross the river and take up a position at Tseng-jong so as to cover the move of 2 Rajput to Yumtsola on 10 October. A platoon of 9 Punjab under Major M.S. Choudhary left for Tseng-jong and established a bridgehead on the north bank of Namka Chu on 8 October. One section of this platoon occupied the Karpola II next morning. Another platoon of Punjab, under Subedar Chhail Singh left for Tseng-jong on 9 October to reinforce the platoon under Major Chaudhary. The Chinese did not react to these moves instantly. However, own observation posts observed heavy reinforcement of Chinese positions. The Chinese strength south of Thagla was estimated to be a brigade plus with artillery support. About 300 artillery guns and mortars had been concentrated at Le. Wheeled guns could also be sighted south of Thagla through binoculars.

It would not be out of place to mention the 'tribal' Signals set up that then existed in the formation. During the three days that he spent at Dhola, General Kaul sent long messages addressed not only to his immediate superiors but the highest political authorities in Delhi. The clearance of these messages was a nightmare for Signals. Every night, the Corps Commander would dictate the messages which were taken down in longhand by Brigadier Dalvi or Lieutenant Colonel Sanjiva Rao, the staff officer from Army HQ who had accompanied General Kaul. The next day, a sturdy Sikh from the Punjabis would run with the message to Lumpu, where the second-in-command of the battalion would pass it on telephone to Ziminthaung, where it would be enciphered and transmitted to Tezpur, Delhi and Lucknow. The first message reached Delhi after three days, infuriating the Defence Minister who demanded the dismissal of the Chief Signal Officer of Eastern Command!

Some of the entries in the diary of Lieutenant Colonel K.K. Tewari make interesting reading, as given below:

*16 Sep. Thinking of problems of OP LEGHORN. Through no fault of ours, we've had a bad name in this operation because 9 Punjab did not open their set. Amazing state of affairs. Army Cdr left for Delhi. GOC and rover group with Ramu (Maj Ram Singh) to Towang. Corps Cdr with 2 Sig Offrs arr today. Orders gone out permitting own tps to fire at Chinese who come into our area. Also evict the Chinese from opposite Namkachu.*

*17 Sep. Corps Cdr annoyed over interruption of his call. He was actually annoyed over late arrival of his ac. Heptr made available for ferrying of eqpt to Towang which had been made available earlier also but eqpt was not then available. The eqpts were help up. Maj Sodhi arr from Shillong with the adv tac HQ of 33 Corps. 4 medium power sets also arr. Another set opened up on C1 link while 4 Div set on C11 continued to work. Had to allot a new area for their medium power sets.*

*19 Sep. 62 Bde arr today. Sent one RS 52 to Towang for our own GOC. Later on this moved to Lumpu. Conf held to discuss the proposal by IGAR for comn. Greasy proposal. I promised to speak to CSO, IGAR. Afternoon meeting at Div HQ. I spoke about high precedence tfc, high security graded tfc, SDS and use of telephones.*

...............

*28 Sep. Long discussion with OC 5 TAC and G staff regarding comn for offensive air sp. All these high floating ideas of standard air sp unit had to be discarded. Finalised the SDS comn for the L of C upto Towang.*

*30 Sep. I was asked to go to Towang. I felt upset. I should be left alone to decide where I should be. The trip got cancelled immediately after when the news of COAS, Chief of Air Staff came. Actually later changed to Army Cdr and Corps Cdr.*

...............

*4 Oct. Big changes afloat. 4 Corps took over by 4 PM when GOC 4 Corps Lt Gen Kaul arr. Gill came as CSO. Plans to move the Regt out of air fd area. I argued s that 4 Div is providing all the comns at the moment not only for 4 Div HQ but for 4 Corps HQ also and least possible disturbances should be caused to the Sig Regt. This had to be argued like mad.*

*5 Oct. Brig PS Gill, CSO for the first time started appreciating some of our difficulties which he never did before as CSO 33 Corps. Agreed to get 10 more cipher staff. By evening, he agreed not to disturb my Sig Regt. Gen Kaul left by heptr with one cipher op at 9 AM to go to Lumpu. Very unsatisfactory for a senior cdr to go and sit alone. It is a very remote place with only one WS 62 comn.*

*6 Oct. Delay in flash tfc last night worrying me. Recce by Gill who saw the logic today of not building around the existing sig centre the corps installations as it would be too congested. .....Flash message from Kaul to COAS asking for air sp against Chinese build up. He talked in terms of national disaster.*

*7 Oct. Stupid message from G1 at Lumpu asking for M Sec and 2 Offrs move to Lunghtu without any other sig staff. This G1 was really a crazy person and less said about it, the better. Let us not to talk about it. I've talked about this same G1 earlier. Then he ordered the move of RS 399 set from 5 Bde at North Lakhimpur to Dirang Dzong to work on D6. ....Decided to open D-3 link at Dirang Dzong and Gauhati with det in 62 Bde Sig Sec. So many flash msgs from Kaul to Delhi and Eastern Command. All TOP SECRET. I can see the strain on cipher and sig centre staff.*

*8 Oct. 7 Bde no comn from 9 PM to 6 AM. Tfc held up. It is a very unsatisfactory state for the Corps Cdr so far forward and moving so fast. 62 Bde Sig Sec completely disorganized. C42 air lifted from Towang to Lumpu. Long chat with CSO Gill. .....Gen Kaul and NP in Dhola post last night.*

## The Clash at Tsenge-jong

At about 6.45 am on 10 October 1962 a patrol ex Tseng-jong reported a large concentration of Chinese troops on the north and east of their post. The patrol was fired upon. The patrol returned the fire and returned to base without any casualties. The Chinese came closer and thereafter intermittent fire continued. At about 8 am approximately 600 Chinese attacked the Indian position at Tseng-jong, which had a total strength of 56 men. Out of this, one platoon had moved in only the previous evening and had not yet dug in. The men had only pouch ammunition. After heavy exchange of fire for about 45 minutes the attack was repulsed with heavy casualties to both sides.

As soon as the attack started Major Chaudhary asked for medium machine gun and mortar fire on the attacking troops but this was turned down. After the first assault the Chinese again formed up for a second assault at 9.30 am. Chaudhary again asked for medium machine gun and mortar fire from Bridge IV but it was again turned down. In the meantime the section which had gone to Karpola II moved to a position about 300 yards away on the flank of the forming up Chinese and brought down very heavy small arms fire inflicting heavy casualties. This unexpected fire disorganized the Chinese second attempt to assault. However, the Chinese brought down heavy mortar fire on both positions causing casualties to Indian troops.

The Chinese were again seen forming up for the assault. Major Chaudhary spoke to his Commanding Officer on wireless and informed that his men had almost finished their ammunition, and that he would not be able to hold on to the position unless support was provided by medium machine gun and mortars. The Commanding Officer agreed but this was again turned down by the Brigade Commander, who informed him that reinforcements from 2 Rajput were on the way. The Chinese launched the third assault from three sides - north, east and west – supported by mortar fire. At 12.30 pm the post was given orders to withdraw. By this time the assaulting troops were on the position and hand to hand fighting developed. Major Chaudhary displayed remarkable leadership and courage in extricating whatever was left of the platoons. He was himself wounded and later succumbed to his injuries. The Chinese had suffered heavy casualties, which were later announced by Peking Radio and Press as 77 dead and 100 wounded. Indian casualties were six dead, eleven wounded and five missing.

It is interesting to reflect on the reasons for denying the Tseng-jong post the support of medium machine gun and mortars that could have broken up the Chinese assault and reduced casualties to own troops. According to some sources, there were several reasons for fire support not being given. Only two 3 inch mortars were in range and only 56 rounds of ammunition were available; the medium machine guns had a limited amount of ammunition; 2 Rajput was moving into Bridge IV to relieve 9 Punjab; the Chinese had vastly superior artillery and would have subjected the whole front to intense bombardment; the presence of the Corps Commander and his party.

General Kaul had watched the action and left Dhola post at 10 am after telling Brigadier Dalvi "this is your battle." He sent a message to Eastern Command and Army Headquarters informing them of the grave situation that had developed at Tseng-jong and sought permission to fly to Delhi to personally acquaint them with the facts and seek further orders. This was agreed to immediately. Before leaving the Namka Chu area, Kaul told the Divisional Commander that the instructions to drive the enemy back were to be held in abeyance till he returned from Delhi. In the meantime, he was to hold his present position.

## Namka Chu and Tsangle

On 11 October 1962, a meeting was held in the Prime Minister's house late at night. It was attended by the Prime Minister, Defence Minister, the Army and Air Chiefs, the Cabinet, Foreign and Defence Secretaries, the Director Intelligence Bureau, the officiating Chief of General Staff, Major General J.S Dhillon and GOC IV Corps, Lieutenant General B.M. Kaul. General Kaul presented the tactical picture of the Dhola Sector at the meeting and then suggested three alternatives viz. to continue building up this sector and launch an attack on the Chinese despite their superiority and a possibility of a reverse; or to cancel the orders of an attack but hold our present positions; or to hold a more advantageous position elsewhere.

The Prime Minister asked the Army officers present for their views. The GOC-in-C Eastern Command was not in agreement with Kaul about the inability of Indian troops to hold the Namka Chu position and therefore recommended the second course i.e. to hold the present positions. The Army Chief, General Thapar, concurred with the Army Commander. The Prime Minister then decided that the Namka Chu position would be held but no offensive action would be taken to oust the Chinese from the northern bank. Nehru left for Colombo next morning. At the airport a Press reporter asked him as to what orders had been given to the troops in NEFA. "Our instructions are to free our country", he said. When asked how soon this would happen, he replied "I cannot fix a date. That is entirely for the Army". Several newspapers reported the statement, some stating that the Prime Minister had ordered the Army 'to throw the Chinese out'. It is believed that the exaggerated version of Prime Minister's statement infuriated the Chinese leadership and was partly responsible for the attack on 20 October 1962.

On 13 October, HQ IV Corps sent a signal to HQ 4 Infantry Division confirming the Corps Commander's verbal orders issued on 10 October that positions along the southern side of the river were to be held at all costs; line of communications via Lumpu would be protected; Hathung La would be held and positions at Tsangle, Tseng-jong and Karpola would he held at the discretion of the Divisional Commander. The next day, IV Corps amended the order, specifying that the Tsangle position would also be held at all costs. On 16 October, Army Headquarters issued orders to Eastern Command to reinforce Tsangle if possible up to a battalion and carry out aggressive patrolling in the area. They were also asked to forward their recommendations at the earliest regarding commencement of Operation 'Leghorn' including their requirements of additional troops, administrative cover and air lift. Apparently, Army HQ had decided that Operation 'Leghorn' had not been shelved – it was held up temporarily until deployment and logistical position improved.

This was a severe blow to the Brigade and the Divisional Commanders, who had been pleading for withdrawal, in view of the reports of further reinforcements by the Chinese and the condition of the forward defences. By this time General Kaul's physical condition had deteriorated – he was suffering from pulmonary oedema and had to be evacuated shortly afterwards. He sent another message to the Eastern Command and Army HQ arguing that the Namka Chu position was untenable and pleaded pulling back the isolated company from Tsangle. To resolve the issue another conference was held at Tezpur on 17 October. It was attended by V.K. Krishna Menon, B.N. Mullik, H.C. Sarin, Major General A.S. Guraya (Inspector General Assam Rifles), and Generals Thapar, Sen and Kaul. Major General Guraya was in favour of withdrawal. Kaul also forcefully argued for an immediate withdrawal. However, the Defence Minister insisted that we should not yield any more territory, emphasizing that it was politically necessary to hold Tsangle. According to Mullik, at this stage he suggested that the civilians withdraw from the meeting to allow the Generals to take a military decision without civilian interference. After a closed door discussion lasting two hours, General Thapar informed the Defence Minister that it had been decided to hold the Namka Chu front and the Tsangle Sector. The Corps Commander immediately passed these instructions to GOC 4 Infantry Division.

The Defence Minister and his entourage flew back Delhi. However, by the evening General Kaul's condition had taken a turn for the worse. Next morning a medical officer flown to Tezpur from Delhi in a special aircraft examined him and decided to bring him back with him. However, no officer was appointed as his relief, it being decided that Kaul would continue to command IV Corps from his sick bed at Delhi. On 18 October he ordered two more companies to strengthen Tsangle. Brigadier Dalvi protested that this would stretch the supply effort of 7 Brigade to breaking point. However, Major General Niranjan Prasad told him that he was helpless, since the move had been ordered at the 'highest level'. When Dalvi protested more vehemently, he was told that he and his commanding officers would be court martialled if they raised any more objections or arguments against Tsangle!

While these high level discussions were taking place at Delhi and Tezpur, the Chinese continued their preparations. Changes were carried out in the deployment of troops holding the forward positions on our own side also. By 16 October 1962, HQ 7 Infantry Brigade had been established at Rongla, close to Dhola Post. The deployment of the Brigade was as under:-

- 4 Grenadiers less two companies was at Bridge I; one company was at Serkhim with a platoon at Hathungla; one company was at Drokung Samba under HQ Infantry Division.
- 9 Punjab less one company was holding Bridge II; the fourth company was deployed at Bridge V/ Tsangle.
- 2 Rajput less three companies was at Bridge IV; the remaining three companies were at Bridge III, Temporary Bridge and Log Bridge respectively.
    - 1/9 Gorkha Rifles less a company was located in the area Chauri Hut above Dhola; one company was covering the gap between Bridge III and Bridge II ahead of Rongla, with a platoon located at Tsangdhar.
- A battery of 34 Heavy Mortar Regiment and a troop of 77 Para Field Regiment were at Tsangdhar.
- A platoon each of C Company of 6 Mahar (Machine Gun) was located with 1/9 Gorkha Rifles and 2 Rajput, the third platoon still at Tawang.
- 100 Field Company less a platoon was at Rongla, the third platoon being at Tawang.

Although the weapons of the supporting arms were in position the ammunition held was woefully inadequate. Only two guns of the troop of Para Field Regiment were able to fire, the other two having been damaged in the air drop. The total artillery of the Brigade consisted of four 4.2 in mortars and two para field guns. The ammunition available at the dump at Tsangdhar was approximately 500 rounds of field and 450 rounds of 4.2 inch mortar ammunition. The gun ammunition had been placed at the gun positions but the mortar ammunition had still not reached the mortar positions. Due to short range the mortars had to be sited about 1.5 miles north of the Tsangdhar Dropping Zone. All personnel were employed in preparing mortar positions and no additional manpower was available to shift the mortar ammunition. One subsidiary small arms ammunition dump was established alongside 1/9 Gorkha Rifles to facilitate ferry forward of ammunition, but this dump had still to be stocked.

While these preparations were going on the casualties due to extreme cold conditions increased. There were several cases of pneumonia, frostbite and pulmonary oedema, some resulting in deaths. The evacuation of casualties was a major problem, especially from Tsangle. It took about four days for a casualty to reach the Advanced Dressing Station at Tsangdhar, with no staging facility en route over altitude of 16,000 ft. The sick rate was abnormally high (50%) among the pioneers of the General Reserve Engineering Force (GREF), which was responsible for the construction and improvement of roads and tracks. Due to the high casualty rate at Bridge V/Tsangle, it was decided to issue snow clothing on priority to the personnel at these locations, the next priority being Tsangdhar. Since there was no snow clothing held in stock, the troops deployed in Namka Chu from Bridge I to Bridge IV were stripped of their snow clothing to meet this requirement. As no porters were available troop labour had to be used. A party of 9 Punjab was dispatched on 18 October with ammunition and snow clothing for Tsangle.

On 18 October a Chinese patrol attempting to cross the Namka Chu at Bridge II area was fired upon by own troops, one of them being killed. Another Chinese patrol found probing the Bridge V position withdrew after a short exchange of fire. As a result of orders received from the Corps Commander from his sick bed at Delhi, a company of 1/9 Gorkha Rifles was ordered to move to Tsangle, further denuding the defences at Namka Chu. By this time, regular reports were coming in of concentration of Chinese troops and stores south of Thagle. Senior Chinese officers were seen holding conferences and pointing to Indian positions. They were also seen taking bearings of all our positions.

On 19 October 1962 a patrol sent out from Tsangle encountered a Chinese patrol on the track to Bridge IV. After a brief exchange of fire the Chinese patrol withdrew. Soon afterwards all observation posts reported unusually heavy concentration of Chinese troops. Hordes of mules were seen carrying various stores including mortars and ammunition. About 1200 – 1500 Chinese crossed the Thagla Pass en-route to the north bank of the Namka Chu. They were seen moving towards 2 Rajput positions and further westward toward Tsangle. It was obvious that the Chinese were preparing to launch an attack and the Brigade Commander requested permission to withdraw the Tsangle Company which was on a limb, out of range of supporting artillery. However, the Corps Commander being absent, the permission was denied.

## 4 Infantry Divisional Signal Regiment & 7 Infantry Brigade Signal Section (Before the Invasion)

After moving from Ambala to Tezpur in November 1959, 4 Infantry Divisional Signal Regiment was faced with two major challenges. The first was the responsibility for communications over a frontage over 1800 Km in mountainous terrain, against the 30-40 Km that an infantry division usually occupies in the plains. The second was the additional responsibility of constructing accommodation for troops under Project 'Amar 2', the brain child of Lieutenant General B.M. Kaul, which was inaugurated in the unit area next to Tezpur airfield by the Prime Minister in April 1960. After the Dalai Lama's flight to India via the Tawang route in 1959, the defence of this sector assumed importance, and 7 Infantry Brigade was moved from Misamari to Bomdila and then to Tawang as the road was constructed. Line communications, hitherto non-existent, was also extended up to Tawang, a distance of almost 200 miles.

In September 1962, the unit was catering for the communication requirements not only of 4 Infantry Division but also Tactical HQ of Eastern Command as well as 33 Corps, which had been set up at Tezpur. The unit was then under the command of Lieutenant Colonel K.K. Tewari, with Major Ram Singh as the second-in-command and Captain A.K. Bhowmik as the Adjutant. The other officers in the unit were Major K.G. Gangadharan (1 Company); Major S.S. Gupta (2 Company); Major R.G. Singh (3 Company); Captain Lakshman Singh (7 Brigade Signal Section - Tawang); Captain A.S. Bawa (5 Brigade Signal Section – North Lakhimpur); and Second Lieutenant Lal Singh (11 Brigade Signal Section - deployed in Nagaland under the operational control of 23 Infantry Division). The Chief Signal Officers of 33 Corps and Eastern Command were Brigadiers M.B.K. Nair and E.G. Pettengel respectively. Other Signal officers located in the area were Lieutenant Colonel B.S. Panwar, Officer Commanding, Tusker Signals; Brigadier P.S. Gill, Chief Signal officer, 4 Corps (after 4 October 1962); and Lieutenant Colonel S.N. Mehta, Officer Commanding 4 Corps Signal Regiment (after 10 October 1962).

Shortly after the incident at Dhola on 8 September 1962, HQ 7 Infantry Brigade had been ordered to move from Tawang to Lumpu. The Brigade Commander accompanied by the GSO 3 (Intelligence) and the rover group left Tawang on 14 September, with the move of remainder of the headquarters and the signal section being spread over the next one week, due to the paucity of ponies and porters. Due to political considerations, there was a ban on using ponies beyond Bomdila, as these were owned by *Khampas,* who hailed from Tibet. This ban was relaxed later and ponies were allowed up to Lumla. The trans-shipment of stores and the mismatch between the carrying capacity of ponies and porters created a major bottleneck at Lumla, where a large quantity of stores piled up. The carriage of heavy signal equipment posed a peculiar problem, since it had to be dismantled, broken into porter loads, loaded on ponies or porters and then re-assembled on arrival at the other end. For instance, the Radio Set 19 and 550 watt charging engine needed five porters each, while the Radio Set 62 could be carried by two. Of course, no load tables had been prepared for such a contingency, it being left entirely to the ingenuity of the Officer

Commanding 7 Infantry Brigade Signal Section to dismantle the equipment, pack them and improvise carriers for ponies and porters.

The move of 7 Infantry Brigade Signal Section commenced on 14 September and was completed only on 20 September, when it closed down its signal centre at Tawang, handing over communications to the signal detachment under the second-in-command, Major Ram Singh, who had arrived two days earlier with the task of providing communications to the ad hoc brigade headquarters being set up at Tawang under the Commander Artillery, Brigadier Kalyan Singh and the Tactical HQ, 4 Infantry Division. Since Major Ram Singh had arrived with no manpower or equipment, 7 Brigade Signal Section had to give him some from their own meagre resources. This included two Radio Stations 499, one of which had been brought to Tawang a few days earlier by Naib Subedar Dharam Singh who had reported to the Section on 15 September, having been despatched post haste from Tezpur, where he was the pigeon training officer of 4 Infantry Divisional Signal Regiment.

Describing his journey from Tezpur to Tawang and onwards to Lumla, Naib Subedar Dharam Singh writes:-

> *I left Tezpur at 1400 Hours. We were four of us - two linemen, the driver and myself. It was dark by the time we reached Bomdila. I made enquires about the road condition and proceeded ahead. It so happened that there was a landslide about 12 Km from Bomdila and our vehicle got stuck and could not move any further.*
>
> *I happened to see a light some distance away and went over there. It was a detachment of GREF, Project Tusker. I explained to him my plight and problem. The Commander of the detachment was helpful and came along with his Jawans to where the vehicle was stuck. They pushed and pulled and with hard labour were not only able to move the vehicle out of the dangerous position but also on to the road.*
>
> *By 11 AM the next day I was able to reach Darang Dzong and got the 499 station loaded and fitted properly in the one ton Nissan.*

*On the 11th of October we started for Senge about 22 Km away. It is a place where the sun is seen only occasionally and it rains for 24 hours at times. The road surface was full of mud, difficult and dangerous to drive, the convoy was accompanied by a bulldozer. There were a number of spots where it was used to push the stalled vehicles. Somehow we managed to reach Senge by the evening. However, by now both my vehicles were without petrol and we could not move forward.*

*At night I tuned the BC 610 transmitter on the D1 Frequency and spoke to the Commander Signals Lt Col KK Tewari and told him about my difficulties and non-availability of fuel. He spoke to Lt Col Panwar the OC Tusker Signals and after that advised me to contact the Convoy Commander. I was relieved but it was short lived as the Convoy Commander flatly refused to give us any fuel.*

*I was wondering as what to do. I had to move forward at any cost but my vehicles were without petrol. The only source that appeared to me was the Petrol Store of Project Tusker. I had been given four bottles of Rum with instructions from Commander Signals to make good use of them and that is what I decided to do. I invited the POL NCO of Tusker for drinking with us. But then I had a problem as how to go about it being a total non-drinker myself. Any way I told my men to join in drinking and made him fully drunk and when he is unable to do anything put him on bed and start filling the vehicles with petrol. This is what they did and tanked up the vehicles from the store as also filled four Jerry Cans and carried them as reserve. I know it was wrong but for a good cause and my move was an operational necessity.*

*I got up early next morning and went to Maj Reddy OC Tusker, well known to me, and requested him to push us up first. He did so and we were on the road. We reached Towang the same day by 1400 hrs along with the 499 Set and I reported to Capt Lakshman Singh OC Brigade Signal Section.*

*He appeared quiet surprised to see the set, wondering as how to employ the same as he already had one at Towang. I in any case was unable to throw any light on that.*

*I have no idea about Towang as I was ordered by the OC to move the next morning with the Brigade advance party with a skeleton Signal Centre. I was totally new to the Brigade and did not know the officers. However, I became quite familiar with them en route to Lumpu, the next location of the HQ, via Shakti. We established communication from Lumpu on D1, D2, as also the Signal Centre.*

Though his signal section had left, Captain Lakshman Singh was not permitted to leave until 23 September, on the grounds that his services were still required at Tawang for the newly created headquarters. He reached Lumla next morning after spending the night at Khillan, a small village en route. He was happy to find that Naib Subedar Dharam Singh had established communications on wireless with Lumpu and the battalions. After rearranging the radio nets working from Lumla, he pushed the remainder forward with the available porters before starting himself after a day's halt at Lumla. Though he was not familiar with the track beyond Lumla, he found no problem in following the correct route – it was marked with an unbroken line of empty Gold Flake cigarette packets, which formed part of the troops' rations at that time! After a back breaking march he reached Shakti where he halted for the night. On the evening of 27 September, he reached Lumpu where he met the Brigade Commander and the rest of the brigade staff, after a gap of two weeks, during which they had been virtually out of communications with higher headquarters as well as the battalions. There were no telephones, and they were using a primitive system based on whistles and flags to communicate with the units, which were located within visual range of the Brigade Major's tent.

Captain Lakshman Singh set about developing communications for the Brigade HQ at Lumpu, hoping it would be the location from where future operations would be controlled. He felt it strange that he was never consulted or informed about operational plans by the Commander or the staff. No one ever asked for his advice on matters concerning Signals and he was not given any orders, verbal or written, throughout Operation 'Leghorn'. He was only told to move to the next location without warning and that too forthwith. Though he was nonplussed by the ad hoc manner in which the brigade was functioning, he could never imagine that not only his own Brigade Commander but also the Divisional Commander were unaware of the future operational plans. As he was to learn later, the situation at higher headquarters was not much different.

As soon as communications had been established from Lumpu, the Chinese began to intrude in the radio telephony nets, telling whoever was listening to vacate the area as it belonged to them. The intimidating tone in which the message was delivered only added to the discomfiture of the users, brought about by the uncertain and hostile atmosphere in desolate surroundings. To make matters worse, most of the signal equipment that began to arrive from Tawang was found to be damaged due to mishandling and needed major repairs, which had to be carried out by the handful of mechanics available. Maintenance was entirely by air, but since a large percentage of the air dropped stores were lost due to faulty parachutes or landing in inaccessible ravines, there was an acute shortage of essential items such as petrol, oil and lubricants. Due to a shortage of jerricans, petrol was dropped in 42 gallon barrels, which were difficult to handle over steep slopes. Telephone cable was dropped in heavy No. 7 drums which were designed for laying in the field, instead of the much lighter dispenser packs. Though a headache for the Signallers, the No. 7 drum was much in demand by others as it could be easily used as a table.

By 1 October the communications at Lumpu had stabilized. Telephone lines had been laid to the battalions, which were all in the same location. Rearward communication on line was available to the Divisional Tactical HQ at Khinzemane. The rearward links D1 and D2 had been established using 19 HP and 76/R209 sets respectively. Another net using 62 sets was working with the rear elements of the Brigade at Tawang and Misamari, as well as the airfield at Gauhati. The signals detachment with 9 Punjab was still at Lumpu, providing a link with the battalion at Bridge 1. As regards the performance of the sets, the old workhorse 62 set worked well during the day with a wire aerial. However, at night the performance deteriorated due to poor signal to noise ratio. The 76/R209, a crystal controlled trans-receiver for Morse code, performed creditably on the traffic clearing D2 link, though it was noticed that its rotary transformer developed faults after prolonged use.

The Commanding Officer, Lieutenant Colonel K.K. Tewari, had already done his forward planning for communications in the area. He assigned the task of extending the existing line from Shakti to Lumpu to Major Ram Singh by 9 October, while Captain Lakshman Singh was asked to lay the cable from Lumpu to Tsangdhar by 8 October. An important document that gives out salient details of the communication planned by the unit is the demi-official letter written on 3 October 1962 by the Commanding Officer to Major Ram Singh and Captain Lakshman Singh, with a copy endorsed to Major K.G. Gangadharan, Officer Commanding 1 Company. A copy of the letter is given below:-

*OP IMMEDIATE*
*4 INF DIV SIG REGT*
*C/o 56 APO*

*Do No 001/SIGS* *3 Oct 62*

*My Dear Lakshman*

*I am writing this to keep ourselves on one net for comns and priority for ops in the future.*

*First and foremost is to get line comn going between TOWANG and HQ 7 Inf Bde. We already have double cable from TOWANG via LUMLA to SHAKTI. Line beyond SHAKTI has still to be laid. This line (for through working from TOWANG to LUMPU) has to be laid by 9 Oct 62, without fail. It will mean a lot of effort and all that with a thousand and one difficulties. As discussed with you, RAMU, we should conc first on laying PVC (double) between SHAKTI and LUMPU. Then we should lay a single line of PVC between TOWANG and SHAKTI and use (for the second leg of metallic return cct), the existing double cable bunched into one. Only later should we think about laying the second leg of PVC between TOWANG and SHAKTI. We should lay the PVC on the ground to start with and then lift it to "Tree Slung" gradually at a later stage. CSO has advised that we should string the PVC up with spun yarn without insulators to start with. I have asked for insulators but they may take time to come. Sleeves jointing are coming up by air to TOWANG on 4 Oct with Lt KV RAMDAS.*

*But whatever happens, this line has to be put between TOWANG and LUMPU by 9 Oct, as discussed with you verbally, RAMU. I know I am asking a lot but I am certain we shall rise to the occasion.*

*Now Lakshman, you have to conc. on the cable line from LUMPU to TSANGDHAR. Your mention to me on the RT about move fwd was confirmed by me with the GOC before he left for TOWANG. You must try and get this line working by 8th also. Again very tough assignment but you may consider laying just on earth return single line, if you feel like it.*

*GOC has confirmed that cable routes in 4 Arty Bde sector will take second priority. I was extremely pleased to note that the TOWANG-PENKENGTAG line has been extended up to MILAKTONGLA and beyond already. This is good show and I feel that the main requirement will be met by this line in the sector.*

*Both of you must consider working of F/Phones on TOWANG-LUMPU and TOWANG- MILAKTONGLA (1 Sikh) line.*

*MANN is at present in GAUHATI chasing the airdrop of PVC and fd cable. I have managed to get 50 coils of PVC also which should be easier to tpt on the ground than drum No. 7. I shall have all future fd cable dropped on drum No. 5. There has been a big hold up on air dropping of cable in the absence of cluster paras and rig. MANN is sorting things out.*

*PVC/cable is now being dropped as follows (in miles):-*

| | PVC | Fd Cables | |
|---|---|---|---|
| | Drums | Coils | |
| TOWANG | 35 | 40 | 30 (W 110 on No.7)<br>45 (D3 on No. 5) |
| LUMLA | 20 | - | |

| LUMPU | 45 | 10 | 45 (W 110 on No.7) |
|---|---|---|---|

*Air Force will not drop at SHAKTI.*

*For pers, we have sent 8 lmn from here, who reached TOWANG on 1 Oct and TUSKERS are making another 8 to 10 available forthwith at TOWANG. They should suffice (as lmn) providing extra man power for porterage can somehow be grabbed. I was pleased to note, RAMU that you have fixed that up.*

*TUSKERS are speeding up the PL route to Jang and then TOWANG. They expect to be in Jang by 12 Oct, with cable up to Jang in existence, we may be able to talk to DIRANG from TOWANG.*

*We are installing our exch at DIRANG at Reg HQ and PL both sides will be terminated on this exch. We shall give 2 junctions to 62 exch in DIRANG. What I am hoping to do by 5/6 Oct is to install ACT1+1 between TEZPUR and DIRANG with BBFU at MISAMARI. All tappings on this line will be removed by this evening. Once the PL is through up to Jang, we shall remove all taps between DIRANG and JUNG also, similarly but that will be later. All this is for your info.*

*Coming to wrls, as I told you RAMU, the GOC is thinking in terms of moving fwd to LUMPU. I have advised him against it in clearest terms. To LUMPU, our comns are NOT satisfactory. Even with C 52 set there, it will NOT be a great help. In any case, it will mean opening D1 and D2 links as well as a Signal/Cipher Office at LUMPU once LAKSHMAN leaves. As requested verbally RAMU, kindly let me know by tomorrow what the final decision is so that we may plan more pers being sent up. I shall also try for another 76 for D2 (for TAC HQ).*

*I want to open D4 link (RT) to TOWANG for reasons discussed with you, RAMU on RT. Lakshman could come up on this also when necessary. This link will be opened in the Regt lines at Air Fd and will be free from interference of other links and other interference at the Signal Centre. We shall remote control it on PL and should it prove successful, we could possible open it as the working RT op link (with existing D1 becoming standby RT/CW link). As soon as you both can, I would like you to test this link out.*

*I am not keen that you should open on D6 from TOWANG. With the tele line to JUNG, we should get that officer in charge of TCP there to keep TOWANG info of all moves on the L of C.*

*Question of wrls sets with bns is what worries me a lot. The inf bns have left their sets behind. I had personally talked to the OC, Adjt and QM of the 2 Rajput the day before they left that they must collect 62 sets from DIRANG en route from GREN store. This was NOT done. Even 1/9 GR could not carry their sets fwd.*

*I hope, Lakshman, your 3 bns are now getting their sets moved up at top speed. RAMU, you may have noted that we have ordered DIRANG Grn Comdr to shift to TOWANG forthwith, 3/4 62 sets left behind by GRENADIERS as Grn stores. I hope no sets of bns are now left on the L of C. If so, kindly let me know by signal. I shall move them up. From 7 Inf Bde there should be only 2 Sets, one each at MISAMARI and GAUHATI and no units sets/left behind with rear parties or on L of C.*

*Can you both examine this holding by units (at your own secs) of 62 Sets, 31 sets and 88 sets and let me have the data by an 'O' sig by return? Check on 19 sets of 7 Bde Sig Sec and H Sec also. I am moving the following sets at top speed to TOWANG/LUMPU:-*

*(a) 62 Sets -6 (2 left by heptr 3 Oct with GOC. (Complete Stas) Two leaving by heptr 4 Oct. Two will follow by 5/6 Oct.*

*(b) SCR 694 -2 (leaving by rd with 2/Lt ANAND on 4 Oct.)*

*(c) 62 Sets -3 (Ex Grn at DIRANG ordered for move on 30 Sep.)*

*This is to suffice; I hope till I hear from you but please give details of holding/loc/serviceability by units so that I can justify my demand for more sets.*

*Out of the above, RAMU, you can retain any two sets for rear links of bns under 4 Arty Bde.*

*All your requirements of teles, adm stores line stores have already been dispatched, RAMU. Anything else you may need please let us know.*

*Both of you have been carrying a big load single handed. So I am sending following offrs up to be used, I suggest as follows;-*

- *(a) Lt RAMDAS - Leaving by heptr on 4 Oct with one Hav OWK and 2X62 sets and 4X300 Watt engines plus batteries. He should take over as OC H Sec with Jem CHANAN SINGH as his 2IC.*
- *(b) 2/Lt ANAND - Leaving by rd on 4 with a 'red' priority for move along with 4x Owl and certain other and other stores. He will act as RAMU's asst for GOC's Gp.*

*Jem DHARAM SINGH will stay with Lakshman and as soon he returns, I shall send CHOPRA as 2IC to Lakshman. I shall try and fly him out (we are recalling ARUN and DK from Courses.)*

*For man power, I hope Lakshman is OK. At TOWANG, we want to keep GOCs Rover Gp separate from 4 Arty Bde, if possible. Details of pers requirements should be sent by you by tomorrow, RAMU. We shall meet your bids somehow. Work them out carefully and give me details. I am sending 6 x OWLs (4 with ANAND and 2 later). One Hav OWK (SREEDHARAN with RAMDAS) and one OSL (with ANAND). These OWLs should be given to H Sec for their rear with two bns.*

*RAMU, I have studied your DOs to RG dated 2 and 3 Oct. Condiments, canteen items, two rain coats (Jungle Boots/Snow clothing are both NA with Ord but I shall keep chasing) and other stores as also signal centre stationery, have all either left or will leave tomorrow morning.*

*Both of you must have seen my 'Y' signal last night about SITREPS. Please keep a special watch on this. There have been avoidable and excessive delays on SITREPS as well as METREPS lately. From TOWANG as from 7 Inf Bde metrep should go direct on 7 Inf Bde B net to GAUHATI within ½ hrs at the most. Give precedence 'Y' to sitreps also and warn the DSO about NR Nos of these crypto for special attention. Sitreps from you LAKSHMAN have been badly delayed in the past. G method MUST (rpt) MUST be used.*

*We are all frightfully busy but not as much as you both and I want you to know that up till now, a difficult job has been handled by you, very creditably. We have some more difficult job/responsibilities ahead of us still and I have no doubt, we shall discharge them well. Do not hesitate to ask for any help, and I can assure you, our answer will be 'yes' invariably in spite of all our commitments here. I shall try and visit you as soon as I can. I have delayed my departure a bit because of all the "brass" arriving in TEZPUR today. CSO is arriving tomorrow morning and I may leave the following the day by rd.*

*I hope both of you have studied the AR wrls layout. With the spare sets now being positioned as required by us, their situation is very healthy.*

*I am insisting that Air Force est their own wrls set at TOWANG. I hope this will be done soon. They can work a link to DARANGA (route of heptrs via BHUTAN) and TEZPUR. We cannot help them on this. TUSKER link to DARANGA is now being worked continuously from 0600 hrs to 1700 hrs daily.*

*Keep an eye on security also. There have been serious breaches lately. Our duty in this respect should be clear in our minds. We are to advise the staff in this respect.*

*Do deep your VHF sets BE 201 also tested. Requirement may arise at short notice.*

*With the very best of wishes, and best of luck.*

*Yours*<br>*Sd/- x x x*<br>*KK Tewari*

*Maj Ram Singh*<br>*OIC Sig Gp with GOC Rover Party*

*Capt Lakshman Singh*<br>*OC 7 Inf Bde Sig Sec*

*Copy to :-*

*Maj KG GANGADHARAN,*<br>*OC 1 Coy*

Lakshman and his men had hardly settled down when the new Corps Commander, Lieutenant General B.M Kaul, arrived at Lumpu on 5 October 1962. With immediate effect, 4 Infantry Division came under command the newly created 4 Corps, which became responsible for the operations in NEFA. One of his first acts was to order the Brigade HQ and Signal Section to get out of Lumpu and move to Tsangdhar immediately. Though the Brigade Commander was not present, they had no choice and many of them left the same night, halting for the night after travelling a short distance in the direction of Tsangdhar. Captain Lakshman Singh could not leave with the rest, due to the unavailability of porters to carry his equipment and was instructed by his Commanding Officer to stay put until further orders. On 7 October 1962 Major Ram Singh landed at Lumpu in a helicopter and took over the radio detachments of D1, D2 and B21 which were then functional. He left Lumpu in the afternoon accompanied by Naib Subedar Dharam Singh and 32 Other Ranks, minus most of his equipment. After spending the night in a *chauri* hut (shelter made of stones used by graziers) they reached the base of the 16,000 feet high Karpola Pass next evening. After a gruelling climb up to the pass they spent another night in a *chauri* hut before moving, arriving at Tsangdhar on 9 October 1962. By this time Dharam Singh had already reached and established rudimentary communications, in spite of the acute shortage of electrolyte for the secondary batteries and fuel for the charging sets.

The clash at Tsenge-jong took place on the next day, watched from a vantage point by the top brass from the Corps Commander downwards. Though the enemy got a bloody nose, thanks to the grit and determination of Major Chaudhary and his boys of 9 Punjab, it brought home to everyone the hard fact that the Chinese meant business. Even as the operation was going on, Lakshman Singh was asked by the Brigade Major to lay a line urgently from Tsangdhar to a place where the Commander was located, near 1/9 Gorkha Rifles, and from there to 2 Rajput and 9 Punjab. Undaunted by the fact that he had no dispenser packs, hardly any cable and very few linemen, Lakshman set about his task at once. All available personnel, including the cook, barber and washerman, were pressed into service to collect the few drums of cable from the dropping zone and make coils for laying by hand. Realising that it was almost impossible to lay the entire length with the cable and manpower available, an unconventional solution was found. There was a line running between 9 Punjab and 2 Rajput, which had been laid by the regimental signallers of 9 Punjab for their company which was earlier at Bridge IV. It was decided to lay a pair of cable from the exchange at Tsangdhar to the location of 1/9 Gorkha Rifles where it was terminated on a 10 line exchange next to the Commander and the Brigade Major. Two pairs of cable were then run from this exchange to the Namka Chu, where the cable between the two battalions was split, and connected to the newly laid cable pairs. The Brigade Commander was now through to both battalions. Of course, the battalions no longer had the direct line between themselves, their calls being routed through the exchange set up near the Brigade Commander. The battalions were not too happy with the hijacking of their line by Brigade Signals, but Lakshman can be forgiven for the lapse. If he had not resorted to this unusual step, it is unlikely that the line would have been completed the same day. In case the Chinese had reacted during the night, as was feared, Signals would never have been forgiven for the fiasco that would have resulted.

After laying the line to 1/9 Gorkha Rifles, Lakshman spent the night sharing the sleeping bag of the Brigade Major, Major Kharbanda. Fortunately, both were quite slim but still, they did not get much sleep. The Commander felt that the Chinese would react during the night to the clash at Tsenge-jong in which they had suffered heavy casualties, and asked for information every half hour or so. The exchange operator sitting next to the two officers would crank the handle to raise the battalions turn by turn, and get the latest information, which would be passed on to the Commander. Fortunately, nothing happened that night and Lakshman returned to Tsagdhar next morning, after meeting Major Ram Singh who had been sent to Dhola Post to contact the Corps Commander, but had missed him. By this time communications had stabilized, and the telephone lines as well as the radio nets were working.

Though the full complement of communications for the Brigade HQ had been set up by Signals at Tsangdhar, there was no staff officer to use it. The Commander and Brigade Major were both located with 1/9 Gorkha Rifles location, from where they talked on D1 net on remote.

As regards the performance of the link, Lakshman writes:-

> *"Just as a matter of interest, while speaking on D1 one morning, with the CO, the signal strength was so good that he refused to believe that I was operating a 62 set. The planning range of radio set 62 was just 25 km, whereas the aerial distance between the two of us at that time was approximately 200 km, he being at Tezpur. Of course, I had the advantage of height. This was good news."*

On arrival at Tsangdhar, it had been discovered that most of the secondary batteries did not have any electrolyte, the porters having drained them en-route to reduce the weight. As a result, two or three batteries had to be emptied to top up one battery. Again, an unconventional solution was found by Dharam singh and his team of mechanics. The 300 watt charging engine was connected to the battery in use, which then worked on float charge, one feeding two sets simultaneously. Another problem was the non-availability of poles for erecting wire aerials. Tsangdhar was devoid of vegetation except Rhododendron bushes, and logs had to be cut from trees about 5 to 6 miles away and lugged up the steep slopes. In the absence of tents, parachutes had to be used as shelters for the signal centre and the radio detachments.

The problem of the electrolyte of the batteries was to have serious consequences for Lieutenant Colonel K.K. Tewari, the Commanding Officer of 4 Infantry Divisional Signal Regiment – it was while delivering electrolyte to the forward troops that he was later captured by the Chinese. Describing the episode, he writes:-

> *"But we were all in for a still bigger shock when it was discovered that almost all the secondary batteries had arrived without any electrolyte. What must have happened (perhaps done deliberately) was that a*

*porter dropped a battery accidentally when its electrolyte leaked out. When he picked it up again he would have found it to be surprisingly light. Word must have spread among the other porters and they may have all decided to lighten their loads the same way by emptying out the electrolyte from all the remaining batteries.*

*How could communications be established on the radio when the batteries were dead and could not be recharged even after petrol had been air-dropped? Such a calamity was beyond anyone's imagination and I had to get the Brigade Signal officer to check and recheck that this was what actually happened. One just could not believe it! How to get the electrolyte up? This time our persuasive powers did not work because the Air Force helicopter boys refused to carry the electrolyte in spite of our good relations with them. And there was no question of dropping sulphuric acid by air.*

*What was I to do? Fate was also pushing me to my inevitable destiny. We filled up a jar of electrolyte (broken sulphuric acid), marked it prominently as 'Rum for Troops' to hide the contents. In another kit bag the regimental Subedar Major packed a roasted pig (we had a piggery in the Regiment) to take to our jawans in the forward area. They had not received any fresh supplies for many days. The irony of it all was that in high altitude areas, all the troops were entitled to get special scales of rations and they were not even getting the basics.*

*On 18th October, I flew from Tezpur in an Otter aircraft to Diranga on the Bhutan border. There I changed into an MI4 helicopter for the hop to Ziminthang. My second in command, Major Ram Singh was already at Ziminthang with the GOC, Maj Gen Niranjan Prasad at the divisional Tactical HQ. After meeting the GOC for his orders and giving instructions to Maj Ram Singh there, I flew in a two-seater Bell helicopter with just one pilot, with a 'Rum' jar strapped onto my lap. We landed on the dropping zone at Tsangdhar in the late afternoon and I marched down to the bottom of the hill on the bank of the river Namka Chu to Brig Dalvi's brigade HQ."*

Lakshman Singh's elation at the performance of his radio links was short lived. On 13 October, he was asked to move to Rongla, the new location of the Brigade HQ. On reaching the new location, he set up the B1 and B21 nets, but could not get through on the D2 net and the daily situation report was not cleared in time. Rongla was located in a valley, surrounded by thick jungle, as was Ziminthang, the location of the Divisional Tactical HQ. It took some time for the equipment to reach Rongla. Even after it arrived, most of the radios sets could not be used due to the batteries being without electrolyte, which had been drained en route again by the porters. After the receipt of a 19 HP set it was expected that the communications would improve, but this did not happen. Transmissions from the BC 610 set at Tezpur and the C 52 at Ziminthang could be heard clearly at Rongla, but the transmissions from the 62 set located there were inaudible at the former locations. With great effort, Major Ram Singh and Captain Lakshman Singh were able to pass a few messages at night, but the Commander and staff were unable to talk on the nets. The problem was aggravated by the mismatch between the different types of sets being used at each headquarters and the turmoil of frequent moves. As a result, messages began to pile up in the signal centre and many high precedence signals were delayed.

The breakdown in radio communications almost resulted in the sacking of the Officer Commanding 7 Infantry Brigade Signal Section. After the delay in clearance of an important message, a signal was received from Divisional Tactical HQ that read:

> *"Op Leghorn (.) h (.) from tiger to tiger (.) information not reaching in time (.) suggest change signal officer."*

Lakshman naturally thought that he would soon be sent packing, but this did not happen. Though the Commander was too pre-occupied to bother about the message, Major Pereira, the DAA&QMG (Deputy Assistant Adjutant & Quarter Master General), prevailed on the Commander not to act on the message, in the interest of the morale of the Signal Section and the feelings of the Officer Commanding. Brigadier Dalvi promptly sent a signal to the Divisional Tactical HQ that he would prefer to be sacked himself. It later transpired that the signal from Ziminthang had been sent by the GSO1 (General Staff Officer Grade 1) without the approval of the Divisional Commander.

On 18 October Captain Lakshman Singh and Naib Subedar Dharam Singh walked half way up to Tsangdhar to receive the Commanding Officer, Lieutenant Colonel K.K. Tewari, who arrived from Ziminthang in a helicopter. He met the Brigade Commander and gave him the welcome news that it was planned to withdraw the Brigade shortly to Lumpu, leaving only a battalion at Namka Chu, with a company at Tsangle. He gave a similar input to the Signal Section, asking Lakshman to plan leave parties for the winter. After spending the night at Rongla, he planned to visit the battalions next day to check on their communications and state of signal equipment. Before he left for 1/9 Gorkha Rifles next day, he spent some time with Brigadier Dalvi when the latter was talking to the Divisional Commander on telephone, pleading for permission to withdraw to a tactically sound defensive position. Dalvi felt that the existing position along the river where he had been ordered to deploy by the Corps Commander was a 'death trap'. However, Major General Niranjan Prasad told him not to flap but obey orders and stay put. At this, Brigadier Dalvi was visibly annoyed and passed the telephone to Colonel Tewari, saying, "You won't believe me Sir, but talk to your 'bloody' Commander Signals and he will tell you what all he can see with his naked eyes." Colonel Tewari then spoke to General Prasad equally strongly and informed him that he could see the Chinese moving down the Thagla Ridge like ants and could also see the at least half a dozen mortars which were not even camouflaged, adding that a massive Chinese attack was imminent. But the Divisional Commander was not impressed. He asked Tewari not to worry and concentrate on his work.

Captain Lakshman Singh accompanied his Commanding Officer to 1/9 Gorkha Rifles, on 19 October 1962. En route, they were amazed to see the movement of the Chinese on the Thagla Ridge across the Namka Chu. After having lunch with the Gorkhas, Colonel Tewari was keen to move to the location of 2 Rajput, but was dissuaded by Lakshman, who pleaded with him to either return to the Brigade HQ or spend the night with 1/9 Gorkha Rifles, the Rajputs not so well dug in having moved to their location only recently. Tewari agreed to stay with Gorkhas, Lakshman rushing back to the Brigade HQ. In the evening there was a request from Major Balraj Nijjar, Officer Commanding 24 Heavy Mortar Battery for a radio set to establish communications with Tsangdhar. Lakshman provided the set and the link got through. In the evening he was a mute listener to the telephone conversation between Brigadier Dalvi and Major General Prasad, when the latter ordered him to send the remainder of 1/9 Gorkha Rifles to Tsangle, and the harsh words exchanged between the two.

The communications set up in 7 Infantry Brigade had undergone several changes since it had moved to the area. On 19 October 1962 line communications existed from the Brigade HQ at Rongla to the infantry battalions and the dropping zone at Tsangdhar, in addition to the Divisional Tactical HQ. The B1 net had all the battalions and 24 Heavy Mortar Battery. The B 21 net was through to Tsangdhar, Lumla, Lumpu, Misamari and Gauhati. The troop of 17 Para Field had also been put on B 21 to reduce the number of stations on B 1. Rearward communications on D 1 and D 2 existed to the Divisional HQ. During the crucial ten days before the Chinese invasion, Lieutenant Colonel K.K. Tewari made several important entries in his diary, some of which are given below, along with his comments:-

> *<u>10 Oct.</u> Flew with CSO Gill to Zimithang by heptr. Changed the heptr at Dirang dzone. Things very disorganized. Maj Ram Singh there at Zimithang while G1 on top at Lumpu, 200 ft higher. Persuaded G1 to shift down next day. .....7 Bde Sig Sec arr Tsangdar in battered condition, after 3 days of march on 5th Oct. Bde Tac HQ at Dhola. Maj Ram Singh sent to Tsangdar at 2 PM. He saw 7 Bde Sig Sec and asked them to push on to bridge 2 to join the GOC – both the GOCs. But they had left.*

> *<u>11 Oct.</u> Gen Kaul soon flew out in Bell heptr. Left from Nellie for Delhi same day. Gen NP arr Zimithang at 1030 by Bell heptr. GOC briefed me on the action of 10th Oct. Frantic msg to 7 Bde to get info. GOC talked to Brig Dalvi at 7.30 PM. Long message from Corps Cdr to Delhi. Decided to lay a line from Lumpu to bridge 1 at top speed.*

*(This was PVC line. Cable was air dropped and Lt Chaman Anand laid this. This was a fantastic piece. I was extremely pleased to see this.)*

*13 Oct. I flew back to Tezpur. Gen Kaul arr back from Delhi. Confirmed own hunch. Further Op on. Gen Kaul not well.*

*14 Oct. Using full persuasive powers to stop move of Div HQ from Tezpur to Charduar. (I was insisting that the HQ if it has to move, as 4 corps had come in, should move only to the airfield). Meeting with GOC 33 Corps, commissioner NEFA, IGAR and DGBR.*

*18 Oct I flew in the early morning by MI4 heptr to Dirang, Zimithang. From Zimithang I was taken by Sqn Ldr Williams in a Bell heptr to Tsangdhar. I reached Bde HQ that night and had a long chat with Brig Dalvi. I could even talk on the telephone to GOC and I had a long chat with him. I remember the Bde Cdr was telling the GOC that Chinese were not there for nothing. They meant business. He was pleading with him to be allowed to move up, to a more tactically sound position. Where he was and where he had been ordered to be – he was a sitting target. He then passed the telephone to me while saying, "you will not believe me sir. Talk to your cdr sigs". So I remember talking to the GOC and pointing out that from where we were we could see the Chinese quite clearly. I could count 10 mortars easily and they were not even camouflaged. I remember even using the term 'like fly buttons all open'. Everything was visible. Gen NP's typical answer was "you stay bloody well where you are. These are the govt's orders".*

*19 Oct. My intention next day was to move upto 1/9 Gurkhas and Rajputs and see their positions. That was after I visited the Bde HQ and checked the bde sig sec pers all of whom had done a remarkable march forward. They were pushed like mad in their move forward. .....On 19th evening I came up to 1/9 Gorkhas. The darkness comes fairly early in those areas. I decided to stay on and early next morning visit Rajputs and then march back to Lumpu. Early morning at 5 am, the Chinese attacked. I was fast asleep when the shelling started. It was very intense shelling. Then, the whole show started.*

# CHAPTER 3

# THE INVASION OF NEFA – KAMENG DIVISION

## The Battle of Namka Chu

At 5 a.m. on 20 October 1962, the Chinese opposite Bridge III fired two Verey lights. This was the signal for commencement of the heavy bombardment by 76 mm guns and 120 mm mortars on the Indian positions at Bridge III and IV; Log and Temporary Bridges; Tsangdhar and Rongla. The Punjabis and Grenadiers at Bridge I and II were not subjected to the hour-long bombardment after which massive infantry assaults were launched on Bridge III, Dhola and Tsangdhar between 6 and 7 a.m. In the very first few minutes of the shelling, telephone lines linking the Brigade HQ with the battalions had been cut. At about 7 a.m., two wounded Assam Rifles soldiers came running to the Brigade HQ and informed that Dhola Post had been completely over run. Fifteen minutes later Captain Ravi Eipe of 2 Rajput reached the Brigade HQ to report that his company had been wiped out. He informed that the Chinese attacked his position from the rear through the Dhola area. At about 7.30 am, the Brigade Commander had a radio telephony conversation with Commander Signals 4 Infantry Division, who was at that time with 1/9 Gorkha Rifles. Colonel Tewari informed Brigadier Dalvi that the extreme left company was fighting a pitched battle with the Chinese there. At about 7.45 a.m.

Colonel Tewari spoke again with Brigadier Dalvi and informed that the extreme left company of 1/9 Gorkha Rifles had been overrun, the company commander and two other officers reported killed. At about 8 am a few stragglers from 1/9 Gorkha Rifles arrived and stated that the battalion's positions had been overrun.

Brigadier Dalvi spoke to Major General Prasad and obtained his permission to withdraw the troops to Tsangdhar, so as to be able to give the Chinese a fight there. Since direct communications with the battalions had broken down, the message could not be passed to them. Brigadier Dalvi appreciated that since the Commanding Officers of 1/9 Gorkha Rifles and 2 Rajput knew his mind, they would automatically fall back on Tsangdhar. He requested the Divisional Commander to pass these instructions to 9 Punjab and 4 Grenadiers who were still through on line with the Divisional Tactical HQ.

Indian troops were completely taken by surprise when they were assaulted from the rear. The Rajputs and the Gorkhas deployed at Bridges IV and III and the area between Bridges III and II fought gallantly but were soon over-powered. There was hand to hand fighting and many casualties on both sides. After having annihilated the Indian positions along the Namka Chu on Bridges II to IV and the surrounding areas, the Chinese directed heavy fire on Indian positions at Tsangle and Bridge 5. The artillery link between Brigade HQ and Tsangdhar that had been established only the previous evening also failed. The Battery Commander, Major Nijjar had been trying since 6 am to contact his mortar positions and the gun positions at Tsangdhar. But he could not get through, as the Chinese had jammed the radio frequency used by the gunners. As a result the guns did not fire a single round.

Of the units deployed on the Namka Chu, the Rajputs suffered the most. They were preparing for the morning 'stand to' (routine practice in adopting defensive positions at sunrise and sunset, when most attacks take place) when they were caught between the frontal fire of the Chinese guns and the main attack from the rear. Their companies were widely dispersed and each fought its own battle, taking on wave after wave of the enemy as long as men remained standing. In some cases, entire platoons were wiped out. The high casualty figures – 282 killed- are ample proof of their valour. Among the dead were many officers, including almost all the company commanders. The second-in-command, Major Gurdial Singh displayed exceptional gallantry. After most of the posts had been over-run by the enemy, he rallied the remnants and led them in a final charge. Most of these men died fighting or fell wounded, while Gurdial Singh was over-powered and captured. He was awarded a Maha Vir Chakra while in captivity. After the battalion had been almost annihilated, the only bunker still holding out was that of the Commanding Officer, Lieutenant Colonel N.S. Rikh, who had with him his Adjutant, Lieutenant Bhup Singh, and Intelligence Officer, Captain Bhatia. They were surrounded by the Chinese and asked to surrender, but Rikh refused. The Chinese threw a grenade, killing Bhatia and wounding Rikh. Finally, they destroyed the bunker with a pole charge. The severely wounded Rikh and Bhup Singh were both captured.

The Gorkhas, who were holding positions on the northern slopes of Tsangdhar, between Bridges III and II, were surprised when they were attacked suddenly from the flanks and later from the rear. They fought gallantly but could not withstand the Chinese assault. The Commanding Officer, Lieutenant Colonel B.S. Ahluwalia, ordered his men to abandon their positions and move to Tsangdhar. He was wounded in the battle and later on was taken prisoner along with a few of his men in the afternoon.

After giving orders to the Brigade Major to destroy documents and follow him with the rest of the Brigade HQ, the Brigade Commander left Rongla for Tsangdhar at about 8.10 am, with a protection party and a few staff officers. Moving on the track along the nullah to Tsangdhar, they came under heavy shelling. They left the main track and started climbing the ridge on the left. By this time, the Chinese had occupied Tsangdhar. When Brigadier Dalvi and his party came to know of this, they headed for Serkhim area through Dhola pass. En route, he was separated from most of the others and was finally left with only Captain Talwar of 17 Para Field Regiment and a few Other Ranks. On 22 October 1962 they ran straight into a Chinese company near Serkhim and were captured.

By the afternoon of 20 October, the Chinese had driven back all the Indian troops from Bridges I to V along the Namka Chu, Tsangle, Khinzemane and Tsangdhar. The brunt of the fighting had been borne by the Rajputs, Gorkhas and Assam Rifles. However, 4 Grenadiers and 9 Punjab had not been attacked. Deciding to pull back the available troops to the line Hathungla -Chutangmu, just after mid-day GOC 4 Infantry Division personally spoke to the Commanding Officers of 4 Grenadiers (Lieutenant Colonel Harihar Singh) and 9 Punjab (Lieutenant Colonel R.N. Misra) ordering them to withdraw to Hathungla. In the event, the battalions commenced their withdrawals but could not reach Hathungla, which was attacked and occupied by the Chinese early in the morning on 21 October. Realising that the Divisional Tactical HQ at Ziminthang would soon be attacked, General Prasad ordered its withdrawal to Tawang. After destroying the cipher documents and radio sets, Major General Prasad left Ziminthang on foot, accompanied by Brigadier Kalyan Singh, Lieutenant Colonel Manohar Singh and the Signals rover detachment.

After covering a distance of approximately 35 km on foot, the Divisional Commander and his party reached Lumla at 2 am on 22 October, where he came to know that the Army Commander was then at Tawang. He could not talk to him personally but was told that he should stay on in Lumla. However, these orders were changed next morning and he was allowed to proceed to Tawang, reaching there at 6 pm on 22 October. However, he found that the Army Commander was not at Towang but at the helipad about 3 km away, waiting for a helicopter to take him to Tezpur. Meanwhile, the Chinese occupied Zimithang on night 22/23 October and Lumpu at 9.30 am on 23 October. With the occupation of Lumpu by the Chinese, Indian troops lost all physical contact with Dhola-Thagla area. This marked the end of the battle of Namka Chu.

## Signals in the Battle of Namka Chu

Captain Lakshman Singh was sleeping in his one man arctic tent, fully clothed as was his practice, when he was woken by a mortar bomb that landed in the Brigade HQ at about 5 am on 20 October 1962. Hurriedly pulling on his boots, he rushed to the signal centre only to find the telephone lines to the battalions cut. On switching on the B-1 net, 2 Rajput came up on the air to inform that they were under attack. Soon after this, the battalion set went off the air. (It was later learned that the bunker housing the Signals detachment had been demolished by enemy fire, killing all the operators). The Battalion Signals Officer of 2 Rajput, Captain Mangat was also killed on the spot. The set was through to 1/9 Gorkha Rifles and Divisional Tactical HQ. The telephone lines from the Brigade HQ to the battalions had been cut, but a portion of the lines from Divisional Tactical HQ that passed through 9 Punjab and 4 Grenadiers was intact. Both battalions had tapped the lines to eavesdrop on the conversation between Division and Brigade. This enabled Brigade HQ to keep in touch with them after the direct lines were cut. Surprisingly, the battalions were also able to remain in touch with each other on radio also, possibly due to incorrect tuning and netting.

Lakshman was soon talking to his Commanding Officer, Lieutenant Colonel Tewari who was giving a running commentary on the shelling going on in the location of 1/9 Gorkhas, where he had spent the night. After 8 am, he went off the air. His linemen were ready to move out to repair the lines, but seeing the intensity of the shelling, Lakshman held them back. Soon afterwards, he saw Lieutenant Ravi Elpe of 2 Rajput stagger in, the worse for wear and almost incoherent. He was followed by a shaken Major Pawar of 1/9 Gorkhas, whose company was holding the forward left flank of the Brigade HQ. He walked in a dazed condition, informing the Commander that the Chinese were just 200 yards away.

Soon after this, Lakshman received orders to organize his Signal Section in 10 minutes and move to Tsangdhar. He asked Naib Subedars Dharam Singh and Arumgam to destroy the signal centre, the ciphers already having been sent with the Brigade Commander's party. The Signals contingent, numbering 40 personnel, set off with two 62 sets, two small 22 Ampere Hour batteries, one pedal generator, one ten line exchange and three field telephones J. With this, Lakshman hoped that he would be able to set up 'hard scale' communications at the new location. Before leaving Rongla, he called up the Divisional Tactical HQ on radio. He spoke to Major Ummat, the General Staff Officer Grade 2 (Staff Duties) and informed him that he was moving to Tsangdhar.

The Signals were the last to leave Rongla, along with the Brigade Administrative Officer, Lieutenant Didar Singh. Naib Subedar Dharam Singh, who was among the last to leave, writes:-

> *The Chinese had cut all the lines and I did not hear anything from Col Tewari. I went to my OC and requested him to move towards Lumpu. I said it was our duty towards our country to put all the Wireless equipment on fire. He was in no mood to go without me, on my repeated requests he agreed and left Dhola Post.*
>
> *I got all the wireless equipment and all the things in one place. I broke all the sets and put them on fire except the slidex. All the secret papers were also put on fire. I was alone with no body there. I had even sent my orderly away. Heavy smoke was emitting from the HQ location due to this burning of documents, which helped the Chinese to concentrate mortar fire there. However, I was lucky to survive. It is reality that the Chinese were just 50 yards away from me.*

Lakshman and his band made their way to Lumla via Lumpu and Shakti, all of which they found occupied by the Chinese. Learning that Tawang had also been abandoned, they decided to head for Bhutan. After an arduous journey, during which they had many narrow escapes and there were several instances of men getting separated and then re-joining, the party crossed into Bhutan and reached Tashinag Dzong Gompa on 27 October. Two days later they reached Border Roads camp of Project Dantak (Tusker) at Beefoo, which was the one ton road head. It was here that Lakshman performed his last act as Sparrow (the appointment code for Signal officers when talking on radio) of 7 Infantry Brigade during Operation 'Leghorn'. Locating a working radio set, he persuaded the Dantak operator to let him use it to pass a message. Flicking to the D-1 frequency, he was able to get through to the Divisional HQ which had in the meantime moved from

Tezpur to Darrang. The operator at the other end was an old hand who immediately recognized his voice. Lakshman gave him the latest information about the Signal Section and the names of the survivors. He told the operator to pass on the information to Major Gangadharan, Officer Commanding 1 Company, along with the advice to change the code signs and ciphers which had probably fallen into Chinese hands. As soon as Gangadharan was informed about the call, he rushed to the radio set, but could not talk to Lakshman, who had left, handing over the set back to the Dantak operator.

As mentioned earlier, Lieutenant Colonel K.K. Tewari, the Commanding Officer of 4 Infantry Divisional Signal Regiment, had stayed on with 1/9 Gorkha Rifles on the night of 19 October 1962. Early on the morning of 20 October he was woken up by the noise of an intense bombardment. There was a lot of shouting and yelling and he could hear men running around. It was dark and he was not familiar with the area, so he lingered, expecting that someone would come and come and call him. After waiting for some time, he came out of his bunker and made his way to the Signals bunker where two signalmen of his unit were manning the rear link radio set. He found that the telephone lines had been cut but the radio was working. He was able to talk to Brigade and well as Divisional HQ and inform them of the Chinese bombardment. After some time the shelling stopped and there was an ominous silence, followed by short bursts of small arms fire. Peeping out of the bunker, he saws khaki clad soldiers advancing towards them. He then realised that all the battalion HQ personnel had withdrawn, leaving him and the two operators. He later found that the medical officer had also been left behind while he was attending to the wounded in the regimental aid post.

Colonel Tewari immediately withdrew into the bunker and decided to lie low for a while, asking the two operators to do likewise. The first wave of attackers passed them. Then they heard the second wave, firing as they moved along, lobbing grenades into each bunker. When the first couple of Chinese soldiers entered their bunker, Colonel Tewari fired his 9 mm Browning pistol, emptying the whole clip. The first Chinese was hit above the eye and fell backwards, being killed.

The second was also hit on the shoulder and fell, wounded. Suddenly several more Chinese entered, yelling and firing. Both the operators were hit, one probably being killed immediately. Colonel Tewari threw down his empty pistol. A Chinese soldier hit him with the butt of his rifle and kicked him out of the bunker. He became a prisoner of war and was finally repatriated to India in May 1963, after spending over six months in captivity.

At about 10 am on 20 October 1962, a Bell helicopter piloted by Flight Lieutenant Vinod Sehgal landed at Tsangdhar which had already been occupied by the Chinese. The only passenger was Major Ram Singh, the second-in-command of 4 Infantry Divisional Signal Regiment. The helicopter was shot down and both officers were killed. During their conversation on the previous day, Major General Prasad had promised Brigadier Dalvi that he would visit him next day, to stay and share the fate of his brigade. The news of the Chinese attack on 20 October reached the Divisional Tactical HQ just before General Prasad was to take off. Finding the communications severed, Major Ram Singh prevailed on the Divisional Commander not to fly to Tsangdhar till the tactical situation was a bit clearer. However, Prasad was adamant and wanted to keep his promise to Dalvi. Major Ram Singh then volunteered to first go himself and find out what had happened, to which Prasad agreed. In the bargain, both officers lost their lives, probably saving the Divisional Commander.

The circumstances under which Major Ram Singh flew to Tsangdhar have been explained by Major General Niranjan Prasad, GOC 4 Infantry Division. After the radio set of HQ 7 Infantry Brigade being closed, it was found that the link to Tsangdhar was also not working. Thinking that the set at that location may have gone out of order, Major Ram Singh suggested sending a replacement set, offering to fly it in himself. General Prasad agreed, deciding to go with him, to keep an eye on the battle and supervise the withdrawal from Tsangle. However, the pilot, Flight Lieutenant Vinod Sehgal objected to the load of two passengers along with the heavy wireless set and its batteries. The choice was either to go himself or send the radio set with the signal officer. Ram Singh argued that establishing the radio set at

Tsangdhar was more important otherwise the GOC would be without communications once he landed there. In any case, it would take the helicopter only 20-25 minutes to drop the set and return. Seeing the logic, General Prasad allowed Ram Singh to go with the set, deciding to go in the second trip.

The death of Major Ram Singh and the capture of Lieutenant Colonel Tewari at almost the same time were a severe blow to the beleaguered 4 Infantry Divisional Signal Regiment. With the Commanding Officer away from his post, the decision of the second-in-command to also leave appears questionable. However, in the prevailing circumstances, the importance of establishing communications with Tsangdhar, where 7 Infantry Brigade was to redeploy, perhaps justified the unusual step taken by Major Ram Singh. There can be no two opinions about his personal courage and commitment to his profession, which resulted in the loss of his life.

Tawang is a small town located on the bank of the Tawang Chu at a height of about 10,000 feet. Its importance lay in the existence of the famous *gompa* (monastery) and the junction of three important tracks that led to Tibet. Though tactically not as defensible as Bomdila or Se la, Tawang had been nominated as the Divisional Vital Ground, which implied that its loss would make the defences of the Kameng sector untenable. The responsibility of defending Tawang, earlier with 7 Infantry Brigade, had been given to 4 Artillery Brigade after the former moved to the Namka Chu sector. The troops available to for this task were two infantry battalions and six platoons of Assam Rifles. The deployment of these troops on 21 October 1962 was as under:-

- 1 Sikh was deployed on the Bum La axis with the Battalion HQ, A and C companies in area Milaktong La; B Company at Pamdir with a platoon at Sumatso; and D Company at Tongpeng La with a platoon at IB Ridge, two km south of Bum La.
- 4 Garhwal Rifles was looking after the defence of Tawang, with A Company located at Tawang, overlooking the track to Bum La; C Company at Landa Village on the track; and D Company

at Pankentang, with a platoon at Gyshie La for patrolling. The fourth company (B) was at Ziminthang, looking after the defence of Divisional Tactical HQ.

- In addition, one company of 13 Dogra was available, having arrived at Tawang on 21 October. Commander 62 Infantry Brigade with his headquarters also reached Tawang by 22 October 1962.
- HQ 'A' wing 5 Assam Rifles with two platoons was at Tawang; with one platoon at Bum La and one platoon at Sumatsu. Two other platoons were at in area Chuna and Dhola.

By the evening of 22 October, the enemy had reached Shakti and blown-up the bridge at that location. They reached Lumla in the early hours of 23 October and their next objective appeared to be Tawang. With the troops at his disposal, the Divisional Commander concluded that Tawang was not really defensible against a determined Chinese attack. He appreciated that the Chinese would by-pass the Sikhs on Bum La-Tawang track and make for Se La by the Chaksang track. If the Chinese blew up the bridge at Jang on the Chaksang track, they would trap the Indian troops on the Tawang side of the river. He decided to withdraw all troops from Tawang to Se La and fight the main battle from there. Major General Prasad met Lieutenant General Sen at Tawang on 23 October and sought his approval for the withdrawal of troops to Jang on way to Se La. Reportedly, the Army Commander told Prasad to do whatever he wished, since he was the Divisional as well as the Corps Commander.

Before leaving for Tezpur on 23 October, the Army Commander ordered Brigadier Kalyan Singh, who was responsible for the defence of Tawang, to abandon it forthwith. Orders confirming this decision were received at about 10.30 am from HQ IV Corps. The order, however, enjoined the troops to withdraw not to Se La but all the way to Bomdila. Another signal from the IV Corps to 4 Infantry Division confirmed it by ordering the induction of fresh troops for the build up to hold Bomdila. In the evening of 23 October, the order was amended by Corps, and the troops were now instructed to hold Se La. This was the result of a meeting held in the office of the Prime Minister at 10 am that morning. When apprised of the inadvisability of holding Tawang with the troops available, Nehru had left the decision to the military.

According to the withdrawal plan prepared by Brigadier Kalyan Singh, all non-essential personnel at Tawang were to withdraw to Jang forthwith, with HQ 4 Artillery Brigade withdrawing at 4.30 pm on 23 October. The withdrawal route from Tawang to Jang would be covered by 4 Garhwal Rifles less two companies and one company of 13 Dogra, while 1 Sikh with one company of 4 Garhwal Rifles would remain at Milaktong La till last light on 23 October. The task of protecting the bridge on the Tawang Chu at Jang and preparing it for demolition was assigned to 18 Field Company of Engineers. However, the withdrawal could not be carried out according to the plan, as the Chinese had already started pushing down the Indian troops deployed on Bum La-Tawang approach even as withdrawal plan was being worked out. However, HQ 4 Artillery Brigade was able to withdraw as per plan and reached Jang at about 11 pm on 23 October. It located itself in the Officers Mess of Project Tusker at Jang, as a telecommunication link with the Divisional HQ at Dirang-Dzong was available.

The Chinese advanced towards Tawang on three axes. A column of about a regiment moved from Lumpu via Zimithang, Shakti and Lungla. It reached the western outskirts of Tawang in the evening on 23 October. Another column of about the same size after overcoming the company of 4 Grenadiers at the bridge below Khinzemane climbed to the Soktsen monastery, from where it took the Sumatsu route, reaching Tawang in the evening of 23 October. The third column of about two battalions followed the Bum La route. This column faced heavy opposition from 1 Sikh, resulting in the award of the only Param Vir Chakra during the 1962 operations to Subedar Joginder Singh. The battle of Bum La merits recounting, being one of the high points of the operations in which Indian troops gave an excellent account of themselves.

1 Sikh was deployed to defend the Bum La approach, its most forward company (D ) located at Tongpeng La, whose No. 11 Platoon was located at IB Ridge, about 550 metres south of Bum La. On the

morning of 20 October, Jemadar Roy of the Assam Rifles at the Bum La Post noticed that more than 1000 Chinese or Tibetan labourers, with digging implements and protected by Chinese soldiers arrived on the Raider's Ridge and started digging. After watching the Chinese closely for some time, Roy informed Subedar Joginder Singh, the commander of No. 11 Platoon of 1 Sikh. Joginder Singh detailed a section under Havildar Sucha Singh to reinforce the Assam Rifles post. Simultaneously, he asked for ammunition from his Company HQ at Tongpeng La. Nothing happened till 4.30 am on 23 October when suddenly the Chinese started firing with mortars and anti-tank guns. As soon as the firing ceased about 600 Chinese attacked the Assam Rifles post. The men fought bravely but the post was soon over-run. After inflicting heavy casualties on the enemy, Havildar Sucha Singh was able to withdraw his section to the platoon position at IB Ridge.

After over-running the Assam Rifles post at Bum La, about 200 of the enemy attacked the platoon position at IB Ridge at about 5.30 am. As the Chinese negotiated the steep climb, they were subjected to intense small arms fire and were forced to retire after suffering heavy casualties. Subedar Joginder Singh asked for more ammunition from the Company HQ. By this time the Chinese had cut the telephone line from the platoon to the company and had contacted Tongpeng La. Even then, Subedar Joginder Singh sent a havildar and three men to fetch ammunition from the company. The party managed to reach Tongpeng La and returned with the ammunition. The Chinese launched another attack on the platoon at 7 am from another flank, causing many casualties. The Company Commander, Lieutenant Haripal Kaushik, asked Subedar Joginder Singh to withdraw, but the latter refused, saying that the enemy would not be allowed to get through the IB Ridge to the 'Twin Peaks' as long as he was alive. The platoon repulsed the attack but Subedar Joginder Singh was wounded and made prisoner. The wound became septic and he died while in the enemy's custody. He was awarded the Param Vir Chakra (posthumous) for his gallant action.

Meanwhile, the enemy prepared to attack Tongpeng La. At about 6 am, the artillery observer accurately directed artillery fire on the steep rock where the enemy had massed for the attack. The Chinese suffered heavy casualties and dispersed. The enemy then made an encircling movement and launched a second attack from a different direction, using snipers to silence the artillery observer. Once again the enemy was subjected to heavy and accurate artillery fire and beaten back with heavy casualties.

In the meantime, orders had been received from 4 Artillery Brigade for withdrawal from the Tawang area to Jang. According to the withdrawal plan, 1 Sikh with 1 Company of Garhwal Rifles was to deny Milaktong position to the enemy till last light of 23 October; D Company was to hold its position at Tongpeng La till 3 pm and then to withdraw to Milaktong La; after D Company's arrival at Milaktong La, the Battalion HQ was to start its withdrawal to Jang, leaving D Company to hold Milaktong La against the enemy till 11 pm.

The Chinese launched their third attack on Tongpeng La at about 11.30 am but were again repulsed. Throughout this day, the artillery observation post officer kept bringing down accurate and heavy fire on the enemy enabling the infantry to hold the position till about 3.30 pm. The Chinese suffered heavy casualties and could not penetrate the defences of Tongpeng La. The enemy tried to bypass the position and attack Milaktong La directly from the east but failed. Finally, D Company withdrew to Milaktong La at the appointed time. During the withdrawal, the artillery officer climbed up the hill and directed the artillery fire on the enemy with telling effect. The battery fired about 600 rounds during the day. B Company of the battalion also arrived at 4 pm and the Sikhs left Milaktong La at last light, leaving D Company to cover the withdrawal. Except for a few casualties in D Company, 1 Sikh reached Jang intact on the night of 23/24 October. By 11 am on 24 October, the entire unit had concentrated at Se La.

In accordance with the orders issued on 23 October, 4 Garhwal Rifles had withdrawn to Jang by 4 am next morning. In the evening of 24 October the sentry on the bridge noticed some movement on the Tawang track. The information was conveyed to the Major Rai, Officer Commanding C Company, who was responsible for the defence of the bridge. The sentry on the north of the bridge was withdrawn and the

Company took up firing positions. The enemy started shelling from three different locations, north of Jang. Indian Artillery engaged the Chinese in the area opposite Jang Bridge and the Chinese retaliated with mortar bombs and rifle grenades. Major Rai crawled up to the sentry on the south bank and saw about 30 Chinese on the opposite side, standing in single file. With the approval of the Commander 4 Artillery Brigade, the bridge was blown up at approximately 6 pm on 24 October by the engineers of 18 Field Company.

After the bridge had been demolished, the intensity of enemy shelling decreased and small enemy parties were seen probing forward at Lao and Rho crossing areas. After this, Commander 4 Artillery Brigade left for Nuranang to join his tactical HQ at Km 106 and ordered 4 Garhwal Rifles to occupy the next delaying position in the area of Bridge 3. The Battalion started thinning out from Jang position shortly after midnight and was able to concentrate at Bridge 3 by 7 am on 25 October. Tawang was occupied by the Chinese unopposed on 25 October, all the Indian troops having withdrawn.

# CHAPTER 4

# THE CHINESE ADVANCE TO THE FOOTHILLS

After occupying Tawang, the Chinese did not pursue the Indians and stopped their push north of Tawang Chu. There was a lull in the fighting in Kameng which lasted a little over three weeks. This was necessitated by the need to replenish their supplies and ammunition and induct fresh troops before undertaking further thrust into Indian Territory. The Chinese had suffered heavy casualties and already extended their lines of communications. They needed time to construct a road up to Tawang to bring up their guns and heavy equipment. The bridge over Tawang Chu at Jang had been blown by the Indian army and had to be re-constructed. To gain time for making preparations before commencing fresh attacks, China issued a statement suggesting a 'friendly settlement' of the boundary question, a copy of which was sent by Premier Chou En-Lai to Prime Minister Nehru, through the Chinese Charge d' Affairs in Delhi on the evening of 24 October 1962. The conditions stipulated by China were such that the offer was bound to be rejected by India. Apart from its propaganda value, the statement was a ploy to gain time for the Chinese to complete their preparations for further offensive.

Together with the decision to vacate Tawang, changes in the deployment of forces were ordered by HQ IV Corps. The responsibility for defence of Se La was assigned to 62 Infantry Brigade while Bomdila was to be held by 65 Infantry Brigade. There were important changes in the command structure of IV Corps. Lieutenant General Harbakhsh Singh was appointed the new GOC IV Corps, replacing Lieutenant General B.M. Kaul who was at that time lying sick in Delhi. Major General A.S. Pathania, MVC, MC, replaced Major General Niranjan Prasad as GOC 4 Infantry Division on 25 October 1962. Major General M.S. Pathania was appointed the GOC of the newly created 2 Infantry Division which was to look after the operations in all the NEFA areas other than Kameng Frontier Division. Along with the Corps and Divisional Commanders, most of the brigade commanders were also changed. Brigadier G.S. Gill replaced Brigadier Kalyan Singh as Commander 4 Artillery Brigade; Brigadier Hoshiar Singh replaced Brigadier N.K. Lal as Commander 62 Infantry Brigade and Brigadier A.S. Cheema succeeded Brigadier G.M. Sayeed as Commander 65 Infantry Brigade.

The new Divisional Commander, Major General A.S. Pathania arrived at Tezpur, along with the newly appointed Corps Commander, Lieutenant General Harbakhsh Singh on 24 October 1962. The Army Commander briefed them about the impending task of defending area Se La-Dirang-Bomdila, code named Operation 'Olympus', which was to come into effect from 10 November 1962. With its four battalions - 9 Punjab, 2 Rajput, 1/9 Gorkha Rifles 4 Grenadiers - having completely disintegrated, 7 Infantry Brigade had virtually ceased to exist. The only troops available to 4 Infantry Division were scattered elements of three battalions - 1 Sikh, 4 Garhwal Rifles and 13 Dogra. While new troops were being inducted, the new Divisional Commander established his Rover Group at Shukla Camp between Senge and Se La and shifted his Main Divisional HQ from Tezpur to Dirang. After handing over its additional responsibility of commanding infantry elements to 62 Infantry Brigade, HQ 4 Artillery Brigade joined the Main Divisional HQ at Dirang. Exactly five days after his appointment as Corps Commander, Lieutenant General Harbaksh Singh was replaced by Lieutenant General B.M. Kaul, who returned from Delhi on 29 October 1962.

During the lull in the battle extensive patrolling by Indian troops along with aerial photography revealed considerable vehicular traffic from Shao to Tawang through Bum La. The rapid rate of road construction by the Chinese made clear their intention to compete the stocking before snowfall. They had also improved the road from Tawang to Jang, constructed a large bridge over Tawang Chu and also repaired Bridge 4. By the middle of November 1962, they had concentrated two divisions in the Tawang area. An estimated one Chinese division crossed the Tawang Chu for operations against Indian positions in Kameng Frontier Division in the second phase. Of this force, approximately one regiment (equivalent to an Indian brigade) was pushed through Mukto Bridge by the evening of 15 November. Elements of this force moved down to Senge Dzong and Dirang Dzong to cut the line of communication of 4 Infantry Division at various places from south west of the main road. Simultaneously, two Chinese brigades crossed the Tawang Chu near Bridge 4 and Mago for operations from the north and east of the main road axis. Of these, one battalion was assigned the task of attacking Indian covering troops (4 Garhwal Rifles) and the other two battalions crossed the Se La Ridge via Kya La to bypass Indian defensive positions at Se La and to harass the Indian troops in the area. Elements from this Chinese column infiltrated into the Dirang valley in the east of Nyukmadong Ridge and took up positions on a dominating feature north of the village, Nyukmadong. Of the other brigade, two battalions reached the vicinity of Poshung La through the track via Tse La.

After a detailed reconnaissance Major General A.S. Pathania felt that a force of nearly 17 battalions was necessary to ensure a coordinated defence of the area allotted to 4 Infantry Division. However, the troops made available were 12 Infantry battalions. In the event, only ten could be inducted before the operations commenced. Of these, five were deployed at Se La as part 62 Brigade; two at Dirang Dzong under 48 Brigade and three at Bomdila under 65 Infantry Brigade.

Out of the three brigade defended sectors, Se La was the strongest, being a natural fortress which was difficult to storm even by a stronger attacking force. The new Commander, Brigadier Hoshiar Singh, had taken over on 29 October 1962. By mid-November, all the five battalions earmarked for the defence of Se La had occupied their defences. A few anti-personnel mines had been laid around the covering defensive positions of the battalions and the Brigade HQ. The Brigade was being maintained almost completely by air. It had about two first–line scales of small arms ammunition and ten days rations stocked with the units. However, only one and a half scale of first line artillery ammunition was held. The battalions allotted to the Brigade were 4 Garhwal Rifles, 2 Sikh Light Infantry (ex 65 Infantry Brigade), 4 Sikh Light Infantry (ex 48 Infantry Brigade), 1 Sikh, and 13 Dogra (ex 11 Infantry Brigade). Of these, 4 Garhwal Rifles was deployed as covering troops between Nuranang and Jang. For fire support, the Brigade had 5 Field Regiment, a battery of 22 Mountain Regiment and a troop of heavy mortars of 36 (Maratha) Light Regiment (Towed). It also had a platoon of medium machine guns of 7 Mahar (MG) and a section of 6 Mahar (MG). Engineer support was to be provided by 19 Field Company

The Dirang Dzong Sector was held by 65 Infantry Brigade comprising 19 Maratha Light Infantry (Dirang) and 4 Rajput (Sappers' Camp). HQ 4 Infantry Division and HQ 4 Artillery Brigade were also located in Dirang. A company of 1 Madras from Bomdila and two companies of 13 Dogra from Senge Dzong were moved to Dirang for the defence of Divisional HQ. For fire support, it had 6 Field Regiment, a troop of 22 Mountain Regiment and a platoon of medium machine guns of 7 Mahar (MG). The Brigade was also allotted a squadron less one troop of armour, from 7 Cavalry.

The Bomdila Sector was held by 48 Infantry Group, comprising 1 Sikh Light Infantry, 5 Guards and 1 Madras. For fire support, it had been allotted a battery each of 22 Mountain Regiment and 6 Field Regiment, battery less a troop of heavy mortars and a platoon of medium machine guns. It also had a troop (three tanks) of 7 Cavalry. Engineer support was to be given by 15 Field Company.

## Withdrawal from Se La

Reports of the Chinese infiltration on both flanks of their defences had reached HQ 62 Infantry Brigade. Troops of 4 Sikh Light Infantry positioned in Two-Lake area had reported on 16 November the movement of more than 1,000 Chinese troops along Bhutan border towards south-east. A strong patrol under the second in command of 2 Sikh Light Infantry had been attacked on the morning of 16 November which clearly confirmed the concentration of Chinese troops in the Luguthang area, on the right flank of the Brigade defences. On 17 November, the enemy had secured a foot-hold on the main road axis by hammering the covering position occupied by 4 Garhwal, which was ordered to fall back to the main defences at Se La. There was a possibility that the brigade defended sector would soon be attacked from three sides and that the line of communication of the brigade might be cut. In spite of this, the Brigade Commander stuck to his decision to stay put and fight the Chinese at Se La. He ordered D Company of 4 Sikh Light Infantry to take up a screen position in the area forward of Nuranang to cover the withdrawal of 4 Garhwal Rifles and 'A' and 'C' Companies of its own battalion from Two-Lake area. Commencing their withdrawal at 9.30 pm on 17 November, both A and C Companies of 4 Sikh Light Infantry reached Se La at 4.50 am. 4 Garhwal Rifles had arrived at Se La earlier, at 3 a.m.

The Chinese had reportedly pushed more than a division through Kye La and Poshingla axis and were using the numerous tracks to by-pass the defended localities on the main road axis. On 15 November they captured Poshingla, overwhelming the two Assam Rifles platoons and the platoon of 5 Guards that had been sent to reinforce them. Orders were immediately issued to 48 Infantry Brigade to send a battalion to Thembang to atop the Chinese and if possible recapture Poshingla. 5 Guards left Bomdila on 16 November and reached Thembang the same evening. Meanwhile, the company at Lagam was attacked by the Chinese and the company second-in-command killed. On 17 November the Chinese attacked Thembang and overwhelmed 5 Guards, which retreated in disorder, some element being able to reach Bomdila, with the rest breaking up into small parties that headed for the plains. By the evening of 17 November, the Chinese had cut the road Bomdila – Dirang.

The Divisional Commander talked on telephone to Commander 62 Brigade, who felt that he would be able to hold out for 5 to 6 days. Major General A.S. Pathania told Brigadier Hoshiar Singh to formulate his plans for withdrawal to Bomdila on night 19/20 November, but not to communicate it below the level of battalion commander. During the conversation, the Brigade Commander informed the GOC about his earlier orders to 4 Garhwal and two companies of 4 Sikh Light Infantry deployed in Two-Lake area to withdraw to the main defences at Se La. The GOC gave his approval to those moves, also authorizing Commander 62 Infantry Brigade to demolish Bridges 2 and 1 in the event of withdrawal from Se La. It was also agreed that 4 Rajput, located at Bridge 1 and east of Nyukmadong Ridge, would come under command of 62 Infantry Brigade so as to cover its withdrawal to Bomdila. On the orders of the GOC, two companies of 13 Dogra were sent to Dirang on night 17/18 November for the defence of the Divisional HQ.

Soon after the telephone conversation with GOC 4 Infantry Division, Commander 62 Infantry Brigade chalked out the plan of withdrawal as follows:-

- 4 Garhwal Rifles was to withdraw from Nuranang and occupy a delaying position at Senge and cover the withdrawal of the Brigade.
- 13 Dogra less two companies with 4 Garhwal Rifles was to cover the withdrawal of the rest of the Brigade from Se La.
- 2 Sikh Light Infantry would abandon Kye La at 4.30 pm on 18 November and take up delaying position at Nyukmadong to cover the withdrawal of rest of the Brigade.
- 4 Sikh Light Infantry would abandon its defences at 9 pm and concentrate at Bridge 1.
- 1 Sikh to abandon its defences at 11 pm on 18 November.
- The Brigade HQ would move in two parts. The non-essentials would leave at 9.30 pm with 4 Sikh Light Infantry and the rest would withdraw at 11 pm with 1 Sikh Light Infantry.

Later, at about 10 pm, the Brigade Commander advanced the abandoning of Kye La by 2 Sikh Light Infantry from 4.30 pm on 18 November to 10.30 pm on 17 November. The Battalion less one company was asked to take up covering position at Nyukmadong, with one company being left to cover Nuranang road. The Commander informed GOC and the battalion commanders about this change on telephone. Though there was no change in the withdrawal timings of 1 Sikh, it's Commanding Officer, Lieutenant Colonel B.N. Mehta, ordered his battalion to withdraw on night of 17 November itself, a day earlier than planned. This decision was taken by the Commanding Officer on his own, i.e. without any orders from the Brigade Commander. It is likely that information about the withdrawal of 2 Sikh Light Infantry having been advanced was probably not passed on to the troops of 1 Sikh. Consequently, when the troops of 2 Sikh Light Infantry were passing through 1 Sikh defences at night, the latter got jittery and began leaving their posts. This triggered a panic and lead to the premature abandonment of Se La.

At about 4 am on 18 November, when the Brigade Commander went to Se La to watch the progress of the withdrawal, he saw that troops of 2 Sikh Light Infantry and 1 Sikh had got mixed up and were completely disorganized. All communications from Brigade HQ to the battalions had broken down or were cut off. Rearward communications on line and wireless was disrupted after 5 am and progress of the withdrawal could not be communicated to Divisional HQ. Realizing that the right side of Se La was completely devoid of troops, at about 5.45 am the Brigade Commander ordered that all troops should withdraw immediately, and concentrate at Senge. These orders could not be communicated to 4 Sikh Light Infantry, there being no communication and the route to the battalion being blocked by the Chinese. The Brigade Commander left Se La and reached at the location of 13 Dogra at Senge at about 6.30 am. At 8 am, the Brigade Major of 62 Brigade informed the GSO 1 of IV Corps from Shukla Camp that the Brigade was on its way to Dirang. He also informed the Brigade Major of 48 Brigade that they expected to reach Bomdila on 19 November after clearing the enemy on Dirang - Bomdila road.

When the withdrawing troops reached Senge, the Brigade Commander divided them into three columns. The vehicle column was asked to move immediately to Dirang Dzong. Of the two marching columns, one consisting of two companies of 4 Garhwal Rifles under their Commanding Officer was ordered to reach Dirang Dzong by the old mule track Nyukmadong – Dirang along the heights and not by the main road, with a view to protect the left flank of the Brigade Column, which consisted of all the other troops, i.e. the Brigade HQ, 2 Sikh Light Infantry, 1 Sikh, 4 Garhwal Rifles two companies and the remaining two companies of 4 Garhwal Rifles. 4 Sikh Light Infantry and section of 7 Mahar (MMG) were still at Se La as they had not been conveyed the withdrawal orders.

The Chinese began occupying the defences of Se La even as they were being vacated. Soon afterwards, 4 Sikh Light Infantry positions came under fire from localities held earlier by 2 Sikh Light Infantry. After repeated attacks on their positions, including the Battalion HQ, the Commanding Officer, Lieutenant Colonel R.B. Nanda, ordered his troops to withdraw. The troops divided themselves into small parties and started marching south of Se La. These parties were repeatedly ambushed by the enemy and a large number were killed or wounded, the others escaping to Bhutan. Among the six officers killed were the Commanding Officer, Lieutenant Colonel R.B. Nanda and the Second-in-Command, Major S.R. Tandon. The section of 7 Mahar that had been left in Se La continued to occupy its location until it was attacked, suffering heavy casualties before being overwhelmed.

The vehicle column of 62 Brigade left Senge at 8.30 am on 18 November for Dirang. At about 10.30 am, when it was 2 km short of Bridge 1, it was ambushed by the enemy. More than 30 all ranks were killed and many were made prisoners. Only a few could escape. The 4 Garhwal Rifles column under the Commanding Officer cleared the enemy delaying position of about one platoon strength in the area of Nyukmadong and a series of enemy stops, suffering many casualties. Just after midnight on 18/19 November when it reached Dirang Dzong, the column ran into an ambush, most of them being killed or captured. The Commanding Officer, Lieutenant Colonel

Bhattcharjea and Lieutenant S.N. Tandon were captured in the early hours on 19 November.

The Brigade column came under fire when they were a little ahead of Bridge 2. The leading battalion, 2 Sikh Light Infantry tried to clear the enemy located on high features on both sides but failed. In the meantime, 13 Dogra, which was in the rear, was attacked twice and could not be brought forward to assist 2 Sikh Light Infantry or 4 Garhwal Rifles. The lack of wireless communication between Brigade HQ and the units led to a loss of command and control and the column was disorganized. The column was pinned down with enemy medium machine guns sweeping the road. When darkness fell, command and control broke down completely and men began dispersing in ones and twos. Some of these parties were again ambushed that night while trying to escape. Brigadier Hoshiar Singh's party was reportedly ambushed near Phudung on 27 November 1962 and he was killed, four days after the case-fire announced by the Chinese government with effect from 23 November. Some idea of the confusion and disorder that prevailed can be gauged from the fact that on 1 December 1962, i.e. after 14 days of withdrawal, 2291 personnel of 62 Infantry Brigade were still missing. This included two officers, one Junior Commissioned Officer and 54 Other Ranks of the Signal Section.

## Dirang Dzong is Abandoned

The Chief of Army Staff, General P.N. Thapar, accompanied by Major General D.K. Palit, arrived at Tezpur in the evening of 17 November 1962. Earlier in the day, they had briefed Prime Minister Nehru about the serious situation in NEFA, where the Chinese had launched another attack in the Walong sector a few days earlier. Lieutenant General L.P. Sen, the Army Commander, was already in Tezpur. However, Lieutenant General B.M. Kaul, the Corps Commander had still not returned from the Walong sector, where he had gone after the situation there had worsened, prompting him to send an urgent signal to Delhi to request for foreign intervention. It was only after reaching Tezpur that the Army Chief was informed about the Chinese attack in the Kameng sector and the plans for withdrawal from Se La. He cancelled his plans to fly to Jhabua and had a signal sent to recall the Corps Commander to Tezpur.

During the day, information was received that the enemy had established a road block between Se La and Dirang and another road block north of Bomdila. The strength of the enemy road blocks was not known. After his return to Tezpur in the evening, the Corps Commander spoke to the Divisional Commander. The latter was apprehensive of his ability to hold out in view of the interruption of his road communications to 62 Infantry Brigade (Se La) as well as to 48 Infantry Brigade (Bomdila). He expected strong attacks next day and sought permission to withdraw his troops from Se La as well as Dirang Dzong to Bomdila. The Corps Commander told him to hold his present positions, though he could plan for the withdrawal if the position became untenable. He was also told that based on the tactical and operational situation, the final orders would be issued next morning. Instructions were also issued to Commander 48 Infantry Brigade to clear the road blocks north of Bomdila. A signal confirming these instructions was issued by IV Corps shortly afterwards.

For some reason, the Divisional Commander was convinced that by withdrawing the troops from Se La and Dirang Dzong, he would be able to fight a defensive battle at Bomdila successfully. Consequently, he had ordered the withdrawal of 4 Garhwal Rifles from Nuranang to Se La and that of 4 Sikh Light Infantry from Two-Lake area earlier. At a conference held at Divisional HQ at 7.30 pm on 17 November, immediately after his tele-conversation with Corps Commander, he ordered that 62 Infantry Brigade will withdraw to Dirang Dzong during the night 17/18 November and will advance to Bomdila with 65 Infantry Brigade and Divisional HQ during the night 18/19 November. The entire Division was to concentrate at Bomdila.

At about 5.30 am on 18 November the Divisional Commander again spoke to the Corps Commander and sought permission to fall back to Bomdila. The Corps Commander left the decision of withdrawal to the discretion of the Divisional Commander, as the necessary authority had already been delegated to him. Immediately after his telephone conversation with the Corps Commander, GOC 4 Infantry Division called a conference at his HQ at which Commander 65 Infantry Brigade and the Commanding Officer of 6 Field Regiment were present. While the situation resulting from the happenings of Se La and the cutting off the lines of communication with Bomdila was being discussed, reports came in at about 7 am that enemy was advancing on Dirang Dzong from the direction of Bomdila while another force was coming down from the hills in the north.

The news of Chinese advance from Munna Camp towards Dirang came as a complete surprise. With no troops at the Divisional HQ to stop the enemy and the certainty of the Dirang– Manda La track also being cut by the enemy any moment the GOC, in order "to save the garrison and troops", ordered withdrawal of Dirang Dzong Garrison to Bomdila. The GOC, along with his Rover Group, left Divisional HQ about 8 am on 17 November. At 8.25 am, Lieutenant Colonel G.S. Sodhi, the Commanding Officer of 4 Infantry Divisional Signal Regiment, informed Brigadier P.S. Gill, the Chief Signal Officer, IV Corps, that he would be moving out towards Bomdila and Tenga Valley and that he would contact him sometime late in the afternoon. A few minutes later, he again spoke to Chief Signal Officer IV Corps, and told him that he would be destroying his cipher documents. Brigadier Gill passed on this information to Brigadier K.K. Singh, the Brigadier General Staff at HQ IV Corps. When Brigadier K.K. Singh said that he wished to speak to some Staff Officer at HQ 4 Infantry Division, he was informed by the Commander Signals that no Staff Officer was available and that he was going to close down at Dirang Dzong. Until this time, the Corps HQ was not aware that HQ 4 Infantry Division had withdrawn from Dirang Dzong. They were also unaware that Se La had been abandoned, coming to know of this only at about 9 am on 18 November when the Brigade Major of 62 Brigade telephoned GSO 1 (Operations) at HQ IV Corps from Shukla camp, giving him this information.

After the GOC had left Dirang Dzong, some officers of the rank of Major and below made attempts to rally the troops into a scratch force to fight their way to Bomdila. But in the face of Chinese pressure, these efforts did not succeed. The men divided themselves into small parties and made for the plains. Like his GOC, Commander 65 Infantry Brigade also left the place immediately without giving any withdrawal plan to his troops. Later, Major General Niranjan Prasad and a few officers of HQ 4 Infantry Division were picked up by the Corps Commander on 22 November 1962 in his helicopter near Bhairabkund.

'B' Squadron of 7 Cavalry under Major S.D.S. Jamwal had only four serviceable Stuart tanks at Dirang. On 18 November in the morning, the GOC ordered the Squadron to break through to Bomdila. In case they failed, they were to abandon their tanks and withdraw on foot. Starting at 8 am, the column encountered a road block in the village of Dirang Dzong covered by heavy automatic fire by the Chinese at about 8.30 am. Brushing aside the minor opposition, the troop reached a wooden bridge which had been damaged by the enemy, making it impossible for the tanks to advance any further. The halted column particularly the 'soft' vehicles, came under heavy automatic and mortar fire. In a few minutes, several vehicles were destroyed and one Artillery officer and five Other Ranks were killed. At 9.30 am the Squadron Commander ordered the men to abandon their soft vehicles and re-deployed his tanks as well as rifle troops, engaging the enemy who was forced to withdraw to the hills in the north. In the afternoon the enemy attacked Dirang village supported by automatic weapons and mortars. The Cavalrymen held the ground and brought down heavy fire, halting the rushing enemy. A similar enemy attempt was made further to the north-west, in the area vacated by Divisional HQ, where Squadron HQ was in position with a rifle company and two tanks. The action continued till last light. Having been badly mauled in their earlier attempts, the Chinese did not come down from the hills again during day. After last light of 18 November the Squadron personnel were assembled, personal weapons and ammunition collected, and the men moved out, abandoning the tanks.

The two infantry battalions at Dirang also withdrew at the same time. 19 Maratha Light Infantry left at 8.15 am after setting fire to their bunkers and tents. They were joined by a company of 4 Rajput en route and halted near Manda La at night. The unit reached Phudung at 2 pm on 20 November. The other battalion, 4 Rajput, could not withdraw as one body as its companies were widely dispersed. D Company, ordered to withdraw to Foot Hills after destroying its heavy stores, reached Bhairabkund on 24 November. The rest of the battalion was to withdraw after troops of 62 Infantry Brigade had passed through their location on their move downward. After waiting the whole day on 18 November but getting no news about them, the Commanding Officer, Lieutenant Colonel B.N. Avasthi, decided to withdraw to Dirang Dzong next morning. However, during the day one company was ordered to withdraw. It left at 4 pm and came under heavy enemy fire near kilometre stone 33. The Commanding Officer and the rest of the battalion left on 19 November, taking the Dirang Dzong – Manda La route. The column of 300 men crossed the Rupa Chu on 22 November and climbed the hill which skirts Shergaon. Next morning on 23 November, the column was heavily engaged by medium machine guns and mortars, even though the enemy had declared an unilateral cease-fire. Being caught unawares, the column tried to extricate itself and in the process killed more than a hundred Chinese, suffering heavy casualties itself. Among those killed was the Commanding Officer.

## The Battle of Bomdila

With the disintegration of 5 Guards after their defeat at Thembang on 17 November, the Chinese were in a position to cross the river any moment and also occupy the Mandala Ridge. In fact, the same evening they cut the Line of Communication and established a road-block on the road Bomdila-Dirang Dzong. When the Corps Commander was apprised of this situation, he ordered Brigadier Gurbax Singh, Commander 48 Infantry Brigade to send a mobile column of two companies and two tanks to open the road to Dirang Dzong. But the Brigade Commander protested that he had no extra force and was not in a position to undertake the task and the order was cancelled later the same night. The Divisional Commander again discussed the issue with the Brigade Commander and it was decided that the latter would make an attempt to clear road Bomdila – Dirang on arrival of reinforcements on 18 November 1962. On night 17/18 November, 48 Infantry Brigade had only six rifle companies, three of 1 Madras (the fourth had been sent to Dirang Dzong earlier) and three of 1 Sikh Light Infantry (the fourth was at Phudung).

At about 10.40 am on 18 November, the Corps Commander directed 48 Infantry Brigade to send a mobile column to Dirang to link up with HQ 4 Infantry Division. The column, comprising two companies of 1 Sikh Light Infantry, two tanks and a section of mountain guns, moved at about 11.15 am, leaving the Battalion Defended Area held by only one company and Battalion HQ personnel. At about 12.30 pm the Chinese launched an attack from the direction of Old Bomdila Pass. At that time, only one platoon of A Company and one section of medium machine guns were in the defences. After severe fighting, the attack was beaten back and the enemy withdrew. In the meantime, a patrol of C Company returned and was rushed to their locality, which had been completely vacant. At about 1.30 pm the enemy launched another attack, which was also repulsed with the help of artillery, 3-inch mortars and medium machine guns. After this there was a lull in the battle for about half an hour, during which all the casualties were evacuated. Some personnel of 3 Jammu and Kashmir Rifles and 377 Field Company had arrived by then, and they were ordered to occupy the vacant position of B Company defended locality.

The mobile column started its advance at midday on 18 November to clear the road-block. The column had hardly advanced about 4 km when the enemy opened automatic fire from the ridge on the left of the road. This fire was returned by the Infantry, but the tanks could not open fire, as the enemy was not visible. The mobile column was ordered back, as it appeared held up by enemy fire. The mobile column returned without suffering any casualty. At about 2.45 pm when they were trying to get back into their defences, the enemy put in a massive attack with approximately 600 to 700 men. At this stage a thick fog set in. Taking advantage of the poor visibility, the enemy surrounded the battalion defences from three sides. By about 3.15 pm, A and C Companies and the Battalion HQ were completely over-run. The Battalion pulled back to lower heights and took up a new defensive position. The Commanding Officer went to the Brigade Commander and apprised him of the latest position. By this time, the enemy had gained control of all the dominating heights and was firing at the Brigade HQ and gun positions. All attempts to restore the situation failed and 1 Sikh Light Infantry fell back to the school building at Bomdila at 3 am on 19 November 1962.

The two tanks, which returned to Bomdila along with the mobile column, were ordered to position themselves in the Circuit House area to guard all approaches from the west. As the two tanks got in position, heavy enemy fire came from the ridge. The tanks opened up on the enemy positions and prevented any further advance of the enemy. The tank commander of the off-road tank put two light machine guns under his tank, one guarding the front and the other the rear. The Chinese, who had thought Bomdila as virtually captured, were taken by surprise when subjected to firing from the machine guns of the tank and withdrew into the hills, leaving behind several dead. This action gave the troops some time to organize the defences.

Having failed to advance towards Bomdila town because of the tanks on that side, the enemy assaulted 1 Madras position at 4.45 pm and dislodged the extreme left platoon. At about 5 am, a patrol was sent to the Brigade HQ since communications had broken down. The patrol reported that there was no one in the Brigade HQ. At about 5.30 pm the Commanding Officer gave orders for withdrawal. The battalion started thinning out at 9 pm and the defences were finally abandoned at 2 am on 19 November 1962. By this time, the enemy had already occupied the position and was exchanging fire with rear parties. When the battalion was near Tenga Valley on 21 November, it was surrounded by the Chinese. About 125 personnel were made prisoners while about 120 were reported missing.

Along with their attack on the left and right flanks of the 48 Infantry Brigade, the Chinese put in a massive attack on Bomdila at

3 pm on 18 November. After the fall of 1 Sikh Light Infantry position, the Brigade Commander found it difficult to hold on to Bomdila any longer. The two battalions - 6/8 Gorkha Rifles and 3 Jammu and Kashmir Rifles, promised by the Corps Commander as replacement for 5 Guards and the mobile column, had not reached Bomdila by 4 pm on 18 November. At about 4.30 pm, Brigadier Gurbax Singh decided to pull back to Rupa, reaching there at 7 pm. When the Commanding Officer of 22 Mountain Regiment arrived at the Brigade HQ Command post at about 4.30 pm he found it deserted. Neither the Brigade Commander nor his staff was there. He heard some one calling on the telephone and on picking up the instrument, found himself connected to Brigadier K.K. Singh, the Brigadier General Staff of HQ IV Corps, who asked him about the whereabouts of the Brigade Commander. Shortly after this, Major General D.K. Palit, the Director Military Operations at Army HQ who was then at HQ IV Corps came on the line. On being told that Brigadier Gurbax Singh was not present, Palit ordered the Commanding Officer of 22 Mountain Regiment to take over command of 48 Brigade in the Commander's absence and organize resistance in Bomdila or in Tenga Valley to the best of his ability.

At about 9 pm, the Brigade Commander returned to Bomdila. He met the Commanding Officers of the 3 Jammu and Kashmir Rifles and 22 Mountain Regiment at 2.30 pm on 19 November. It was felt that unless the new troops had reconnoitred the area, an immediate attack on the enemy was inadvisable. The Brigade Commander again ordered all troops to withdraw from Bomdila. He left for Rupa, reaching there at dawn on dawn on 19 November. The troops finally left Bomdila at 5.15 am on 19 November.

The Corps Commander, when he came to know of the withdrawal of troops from Bomdila, sent a special message through Major Nahar Singh, Signal Officer of Tusker Force, for the Commander 48 Infantry Brigade, ordering him to occupy the defences at Rupa. The Brigade Commander ordered 1 Sikh Light Infantry to occupy a high ground near Rupa. At about 8 am, when the battalion was getting ready to move, the Chinese opened up with automatics from all the features around the Rupa defile. By that time, troops of 6/8 Gorkha Rifles, which had returned to Tenga Valley in the early morning in vehicles, were on their way back to Rupa. They were caught in the enemy fire in the Rupa gap and became disorganized. At this stage, Brigadier Gurbax Singh again ordered withdrawal along the high ground on either side of the Rupa valley.

The Commanding Officer of 6/8 Gorkha Rifles was ordered to position his troops in a narrow defile, approximately 2 km south of Rupa gap, until all units of the Brigade had passed through. The battalion held the gap until midday on 19 November, when the Brigade Commander ordered that the troops should withdraw from Rupa to Chako to foil a possible Chinese attempt to cut off the entire force there. However, the enemy continued following up the withdrawing troops. 3 Jammu and Kashmir Rifles, which withdrew from Bomdila directly to Tenga Valley, came under heavy enemy fire from the opposite ridge at about 9 am. The battalion suffered heavy casualties and broke up, some elements withdrawing to Chako, while the rest moving directly to Tezpur.

When 48 Infantry Brigade reached Chako at last light on 19 November, it was already growing dark. Brigadier Gurbax Singh sent for ammunition, digging tools and rations which started arriving. The troops were still busy preparing their trenches when, at about 2.45 am on 20 November, they came under heavy enemy fire from the surrounding heights. Soon afterwards, the position was attacked at different places along the perimeter. Meanwhile, the stores continued to arrive. Unfortunately, at 3.15 a.m. a vehicle carrying ammunition overturned and blocked the road. The Sikh Light Infantry troops, who were on the high ground astride Chako Check post, had to pull back as their ammunition got exhausted. After this the Chinese surrounded the 6/8 Gorkha Rifles positions. By 3.30 am, two attempts by the enemy to break into their defences had been thwarted. But the Battalion HQ was overrun by the enemy at about 3.45 am. Although they continued to suffer casualties, the Gorkhas held on to their respective positions tenaciously till 5.30 am, when the Commanding Officer ordered them to withdraw to Foot Hills. Till 1 December 1962, more than 150 all ranks were still missing.

## The Aftermath

The withdrawal from Se La marks an ignominious chapter in India's military history, and has given rise to considerable debate. The Henderson-Brookes Enquiry questioned a large number of personnel who played a part in the decision to vacate Se La, but its report has still not been de-classified. There is considerable variation in the versions of officers who wrote books after the event, as well the war diaries of various formations and units. However, it is possible arrive at certain conclusions regarding the circumstances that led to the withdrawal, even though the Brigade Commander was dead against it. Significantly, Signals played a part in the story.

According to Major General A.S. Pathania, GOC 4 Infantry Division, his decision to withdraw from Se La was based on an input from Brigadier Hoshiar Singh, Commander 62 Infantry Brigade on the evening of 17 November that his defences had become untenable. However, the decision had already been taken by the GOC before the conversation took place and everyone in the Divisional HQ knew that they were to move back to Tenga valley, south of Bomdila. At 3 pm on 17 November Lieutenant Colonel G.S. Sodhi, Commander Signals 4 Infantry Division spoke to Brigadier P.S. Gill, Chief Signal Officer of IV Corps and informed him that at 4.30 pm he would be moving out with the lay out group for the purpose of establishing the Divisional HQ at the new location. In fact, a staff officer from the Divisional HQ had already been sent to Tenga, where HQ 4 Infantry Division was initially planned to be moved. However, after the fall of Thembang and the establishment of a road block between Bomdila and Dirang Dzong in the afternoon, the plan to move to Tenga was shelved and the officer was called back.

During his conversation with Brigadier Gill, Lieutenant Colonel Sodhi told him that his GOC wanted to speak to the Corps

Commander. When he was told that the Corps Commander was not present – he had gone to Walong – he spoke to the Brigadier K.K. Singh, the Brigadier General Staff and requested for permission to withdraw from Se La. In the absence of the Corps Commander, Brigadier K.K. Singh expressed his inability to give the permission for withdrawal and advised him to hold on. Later, when the Chief of Army Staff, the Army Commander and the Director Military Operations arrived at the Corps HQ, Brigadier K.K. Singh informed them about his conversation with GOC 4 Infantry Division and the latter's request for withdrawal. While Brigadier K.K. Singh was briefing the Army Chief and the Army Commander, GOC 4 Infantry Division again telephoned with an urgent request for permission to withdraw, which was again denied. Subsequently, Major General Pathania spoke to Brigadier Hoshiar Singh and suggested that he should withdraw from Se La the same night. Brigadier Hoshiar Singh protested, since he was confident that his defences were strong enough to repel an attack by the enemy. Finally, he agreed to withdraw the next night, i.e. the night of 18/19 November. It was after this conversation that Brigadier Hoshiar Singh informed his Battalion Commanders about the withdrawal from Se La during night 18/19 November.

At about 7 pm, the Corps Commander returned to Tezpur from his trip to Walong. After talking to the Divisional Commander and discussing the situation with the Chief and the Army Commander, he ordered a signal to be sent to 4 Infantry Division to withdraw to Bomdila. Brigadier Gill recalls that the signal was given at about 7 pm. Since the signal was classified, it had to be enciphered before transmission and deciphered at the other end. To save time, Brigadier K.K. Singh telephoned Commander 48 Infantry Brigade at Bomdila and asked him to pass the message to GOC 4 Infantry Division on telephone. After encryption, the signal was transmitted to Bomdila for onward transmission to the Divisional HQ. Apparently, after discussion with the Chief and the Army Commander, Lieutenant General Kaul changed his mind, and ordered that the signal should be cancelled. Brigadier K.K. Singh again telephoned Brigadier Gurbax Singh at Bomdila and asked him not to pass the message he had given to him earlier, regarding the withdrawal of 4 Infantry Division. Brigadier Gurbax Singh confirmed that the message had not been passed since the telephone line between Bomdila and Dirang was out of order.

After the cancellation of the above signal, General Kaul gave another hand written signal to Brigadier K.K. Singh to be passed on to GOC 4 Infantry Division, directing him to hold on to his present positions to the best of his ability. However, if any position became untenable, the Divisional Commander was delegated the authority to withdraw to any alternate position he could hold. The message was cleared to HQ 4 Infantry Division at about 2.30 am on 18 November 1962.

At about 10.30 pm on 17 November, Commander 62 Infantry Brigade telephoned the GOC to inform him about the latest situation in his Brigade. Major General Pathania told Brigadier Hoshiar Singh that he could make his withdrawal plan but final orders would be given in the morning. But the situation changed during the night, when 2 Sikh Light Infantry was pulled out of Kye La at about 10.30 pm that night, triggering the pre mature withdrawal of 1 Sikh without orders. 2 Sikh Light Infantry was withdrawn according to plan and not because of enemy pressure. The GOC was informed by the Brigade Commander regarding this step. If 1 Sikh had not withdrawn on their own, it is unlikely that Se la would have been abandoned on the night of 17/18 November, setting off the alarm that resulted in the panic stricken flight of the troops of 62 Infantry Brigade from Se La.

After the fall of Chako, all semblance of any defence ended. The famous Red Eagle Division, which had won universal acclaim for its victories in World War II had been virtually destroyed. After the fall of Se La and Bomdila, all command and control was lost. Proud battalions had crumbled into small parties, some heading for the foot hills and others to Bhutan. This caused panic and bewilderment in the rear areas also. Because of lack of communications with HQ 4 Infantry Division or any of its subordinate formations or units, there was no precise information about either the casualties or missing men. Even on 30 November, ten days after the fall of Bomdila, the number of personnel listed as missing was 119 officers, 143 Junior Commissioned Officers and 5431 Other Ranks.

Alarmed by the debacles at Se la and Bomdila, and developing threat to Tezpur, Army HQ ordered 5 Infantry Division to be airlifted from Punjab, for the defence of Tezpur. The advance party of HQ 5 Infantry Division along with one Brigade HQ and one Infantry battalion landed at Tezpur on 19 November and began to dig in for the defence of Tezpur airfield. On 20 November the situation at Tezpur was completely out of control after a part of HQ IV Corps left for Gauhati. Rumours started that the Army was vacating Assam, leaving the civilians at the mercy of the Chinese who were expected to reach the plains in a matter of days. With the anticipated departure of the military, the civilian administration panicked and the District Magistrate left for Gauhati. Law and order collapsed and the jail was thrown open, releasing all prisoners. The district treasury office was ordered to burn currency to prevent it falling into Chinese hands. All government offices started burning documents, creating a thick pall of smoke over the city. By nightfall, Tezpur became a ghost city.

On 21 November 1962, the Chinese declared a cease-fire. Soon afterwards, General Thapar retired on health grounds, though he had offered to resign. General J.N. Chaudhury, the GOC-in-C Southern Command, was appointed the new Chief of Army Staff. Lieutenant General B.M. Kaul resigned, being succeeded by Lieutenant General S.H.F.J. Manekshaw, who moved on promotion from his appointment as Commandant of the Defence Services Staff College at Wellington. The Defence Minister, V.K Krishna Menon also lost his job. Though Nehru was reluctant to remove him, he bowed to vociferous demands for his removal in Parliament and the Press. The debacle affected Nehru also. He was a broken man, his unquestioned authority eroded after 1962. He did not live long, breathing his last in May 1964, exactly a year and a half after the Chinese invasion.

# CHAPTER 5

# THE INVASION OF NEFA–WALONG SECTOR

Other than Kameng, the only part of NEFA invaded by the Chinese was Walong in the Lohit Frontier Division. Incursions did take place in Subansiri and Siang divisions of NEFA and along the Indo-Tibet border areas in Uttar Pradesh and Himachal Pradesh, but these were minor and did not involve significant fighting. Even in Walong, the number of troops involved was small, in comparison to those that took part in the operations in Kameng. However, the heavy casualties incurred by both sides bear testimony to the intensity of the conflict, and merit recounting.

Before the responsibility for the defence of NEFA was handed over to the Army in 1959, only 2 Assam Rifles was deployed in the Lohit Division, with a wing each at Dibang Valley, Hayuliang and Walong. A regular battalion – 2 Rajput – was located at Walong only in July 1961. In April 1962, 6 Kumaon took over the responsibility for the defence of the area. With the launching of Operation 'Onkar' which envisaged setting up of additional posts by Assam Rifles, under the operational control of the Army, eleven new posts were set up in Lohit Frontier Division. In September 1962 two battalions of 62 Infantry Brigade – 4 Sikh and 2/8 Gorkha Rifles - were moved from Ramgarh to Jorhat and placed under 5 Infantry Brigade. 4 Sikh, which was earmarked for the Lohit Frontier Division, arrived at Walong on 8 October 1962.

On 18 October 1962, the deployment of Indian troops in the three sub sectors was as under:-

- Dibang Valley sub-sector - 2 Assam Rifles
- Kibithoo sub-sector - 6 Kumaon.
- Walong sub sector – 4 Sikh less two companies.

By this time the Chinese strength on NEFA-Tibet border had gone up to nineteen battalions, of which six were positioned opposite the Lohit Frontier Division. In September 1962 Chinese troops had moved closer to the border and had been observed digging and preparing defensive positions opposite Indian posts. According intelligence estimates of HQ IV Corps, the Chinese had deployed one infantry division in area Shugden – Drowa Gompa – Tithang. Shugden was on the main Lhasa-Chamdo highway, from where Rima could be approached via two routes, Shugden – Drowa Gompa – Rima and Shugden – Tithang – Rima. The Chinese were known to have improved the Drowa Gompa – Rima road that led to Kibithoo and onwards to Walong on the Indian side of the border.

## Fall of Kibithoo

Located on the western bank of the Lohit River, Kibithoo was held by 6 Kumaon with the Battalion HQ at Walong and tactical HQ at Kibithoo. A reconnaissance patrol sent on 18 October 1962 to a feature known as Hundred Hill observed the presence of some enemy soldiers on the feature. Next morning, an Assam Rifles platoon was sent to the feature to check the Chinese advance to Kibithoo along that approach. A platoon of 'A' Company of 6 Kumaon was also sent to take up position on the McMahon Ridge followed by the whole Company on 21 October. A platoon was also sent up along Di Chu Nullah to prevent any enemy advance from Taluk Pass. On the same night, after a preparatory bombardment by medium machine guns and artillery, the enemy attacked the McMahon Ridge with approximately a battalion group. The first attack was repulsed by accurate firing by the battalion's 3-inch mortars, which were positioned south-west of Kibithoo Ridge.

After some time, the Chinese launched another violent attack. The Kumaonis stuck to their position and held the enemy at bay, with accurate fire from small arms and mortars. About 60 Chinese were killed in this action, the Indian losses being four killed. However, in view of the considerable numerical superiority of the enemy and lack of reinforcements, it was decided to withdraw A Company from the McMahon Ridge and Di Chu and concentrate at Kibithoo. The troops started withdrawing at 7 am on 22 October.

The Brigade Commander arrived at Walong at 9 am to personally review the situation. After talking to the Commanding Officer of 6 Kumaon on telephone, he gave orders to cut all the twine rope-ways across the Lohit River at Kibithoo. The enemy continued his shelling using smoke bombs, causing dense smoke in the whole area. At 10 am on 22 October 1962, HQ 5 Infantry Brigade received orders placing it directly under IV Corps. In view of the loss of the Dichu Ridge and enemy build up against Kibithoo, IV Corps ordered the withdrawal of 6 Kumaon from Kibithoo, and occupation of a new defensive position at Walong, along with 4 Sikh. At the same time, all Assam Rifle posts on the western side were to be withdrawn to Hayuliang for protection of the left flank of Walong Garrison. In response to the order, 6 Kumaon abandoned Kibithoo at 9 pm on 22 October 1962 and concentrated at Walong by 5 pm on 23 October 1962.

Shortly afterwards, 2 Infantry Division was raised to take over operational responsibility in Subansiri, Siang and Lohit Frontier Divisions of NEFA. The first Divisional Commander, Major General M.S. Pathania, arrived at Walong on 26 October. In order to control the two battalions located at Walong, 181 Infantry Brigade was raised. This was replaced by 11 Infantry Brigade, then in Nagaland, which was placed under 2 Infantry Division. The Brigade Commander, Brigadier N.C. Rawlley, MC, along with his Rover Group arrived at Walong at on 31 October. On 31 October 1962, the Brigade comprised 6 Kumaon, 4 Sikh, two companies of 2/8 Gorkha Rifles and one company of 3/3 Gorkha Rifles. Supporting troops were a platoon 6 Mahar MG, a troop of 62 Para Field Battery and 71 Heavy Mortar Battery.

After the withdrawal of Indian troops from Kibithoo, the Chinese had occupied positions behind Ashi Hill. Since then it had become a daily routine for the Chinese troops to fire at the Mithun and Ladders positions and also to carry out probing attacks on Indian defences. This exchange of fire was so regular that Indian troops from other posts used to visit the Mithun-Ladders area daily to witness the 'fire works', to amuse themselves. The Indian firing taxed the Chinese so heavily that on 2 November the local commander sent a message to the rear for permission to withdraw, which was refused, since the Chinese did not like to lose face. The Chinese fire on the Mithun and Ladders positions was, in fact, a ruse to cover their activities somewhere else. Behind the screen of their firing, the Chinese constructed a track from Ashi Hill to the Green Pimple post and started their build-up unchecked.

## Battle of Walong

To check the enemy incursion Commander 11 Infantry Brigade decided to occupy the area Tri-junction – Yellow Pimple – Green Pimple which were crucial to the defence of Walong. Additional troops allotted to the Brigade for the offensive were 3/3 Gorkha Rifles and 4 Dogra. By 13 November Tri-junction had been occupied by 6 Kumaon, while 4 Sikh was on the forward slopes of West Ridge and Ladders. The newly arrived 3/3 Gorkha was deployed on Dakota Hill and the Dong Plateau, while 4 Dogra was still in the process of being inducted, most of its elements at Walong.

The attack on Yellow Pimple was launched by 6 Kumaon on 14 November. The enemy reacted violently and by nightfall the Kumaonis had been able to capture only a part of the feature. Next morning, the Chinese counter attacked with a battalion supported by artillery. After fierce hand to hand fighting the Kumaonis were forced to fall back to Tri-Junction, after losing 110 men out of the 200 who had taken part in the assault the previous day. Not pausing on the recaptured objective, the Chinese attacked Tri-Junction, where the troops had withdrawn from on Yellow Pimple. After a bitter fight lasting over two hours the attack was repulsed.

The Chinese launched a massive attack on Tri-Junction at 7.30 am on 16 November, which was beaten back. However, the position was completely surrounded, and the enemy had cut off the routes of replenishment and reinforcement and the number of casualties was mounting, with no hope of evacuation. Realising that further resistance was useless, the Commanding Officer, Lieutenant Colonel Madiah decided to disengage and withdraw his troops. Tri-Junction was occupied by the enemy at 9 am on 16 November. As they withdrew, the Kumaonis were repeatedly ambushed by the enemy on their downward march.

The West ridge was held by A Company of 6 Kumaon, which was attacked by the Chinese after they had overcome the Indian defences at Tri-Junction. The first assault mounted frontally failed. The next attack was made with larger numbers from three directions, supported by medium machine guns and heavy artillery. After holding out for several hours, the Company found itself encircled and asked for permission to withdraw. One Junior Commissioned Officer and 17 Other Ranks were able to break through the Chinese ring, but the rest died fighting including the Company Commander, Lieutenant Bikram Singh.

Similar attacks were launched by the Chinese on other posts. They attacked Patrol Base which was held by A Company of 4 Sikh at 9 pm on 15 November. With the help of artillery fire, the attack was repulsed. The Chinese attacked the position several times during the night, being beaten back on each occasion. After fighting resolutely throughout the night, the company asked for and was given permission to withdraw to the Maha Plateau. During the withdrawal, the Company Commander was killed. The casualties suffered by the Sikhs during the operation were one officer, one Junior Commissioned Officer and 20 Other Ranks killed, while two Junior Commissioned Officers and 40 Other Ranks were wounded. Among those killed were four Olympic sportsmen.

One of the fiercest battles was fought at Ladders which was being held by C Company of 3/3 Gorkha Rifles under command 4 Sikh. At about 3 am on 16 November, the Chinese attacked Ladders after destroying the bunkers occupied by the Gorkhas. The Company

Commander, Major N.B. Chand ordered his men to come out into the crawl trenches to fight the enemy. The situation became critical when small groups of enemy started infiltrating to the Indian gun positions under small arms fire. The Company Commander requested 4 Sikh for reinforcements and ammunition, which could not be sent. Finally the position was abandoned. After his bunker was destroyed, the Company Commander found himself alone. He was later captured by the Chinese.

Maha Plateau, Lachhman Ridge and the Mithun track were held by C Company of 4 Sikh and D Company of 3/3 Gorkha Rifles, under command 4 Sikh. After over-running the Patrol Base on 16 November, the Chinese advanced and launched attacks on these positions, which were overrun and the troops dispersed, both company commanders being captured.

The High Plateau on the right extremity of the Walong Front was held by D Company of 4 Sikh under the operational command of 3/3 Gorkha Rifles. At 11.30 pm on 15 November a strong enemy force attacked the position but was beaten back. The second attack came at about 1.30 am on 16 November during which the Company Commander, Lieutenant Yog Raj Palta was killed. After the death of Lieutenant Palta, Havildar Gurmukh Singh took over command, when only 18 men were left in the company. At 4.45 am the Chinese launched the third attack overwhelming the position. The Sikhs lost 36 men including the Company Commander. During the early hours of the day, efforts were made to reinforce the Sikhs, but the Gorkhas could not go beyond the southern edge of High Plateau. At about 8 am the artillery observation post officer, Second Lieutenant P.S. Bhandari reached the post and assumed command of the few non-combatant Sikhs who were still alive. For some time he directed artillery fire on the Chinese but was soon killed. When the Chinese captured the position there was not a single Indian soldier left alive.

The battle for the capture of Yellow Pimple was witnessed by the Brigade Commander, Brigadier N.C. Rawlley on 14 November. The Corps Commander and the Divisional Commander were at Walong with the Brigade Commander from the afternoon of 15 November till they left Walong for Hayuliang by an Otter aircraft at 11 am on 16 November. While leaving Walong, Lieutenant General Kaul instructed the Brigade Commander to hold the Defended Sector to the best of his ability. However, if the position became untenable, he was to fall back to an alternative position. These orders were confirmed by HQ IV Corps to 11 Infantry Brigade in the evening, through a signal.

After launching attacks on Indian positions all along the front the enemy had secured a foothold both on the western and eastern side of the Lohit River and was in a position to shell the Walong landing ground. Out of the four battalions that it had, only four companies (two of 3/3 Gorkha Rifles at Dong Plateau and two of 4 Dogra at Brigade HQ) were left of 11 Infantry Brigade. With his fighting strength severely depleted, the Brigade Commander, at 11 am on 16 November, gave orders for the withdrawal of troops from the forward areas and for the holding of Yapak feature. The troops at Tri-Junction and Mortar Post had already disintegrated before they received the orders for withdrawal at about 12 pm. They could not carry out an organized withdrawal due to the pressure from the enemy. They moved in small parties and the troops kept on trickling down to Tezu, till 4 December 1962. The casualties suffered by 6 Kumaon in the operations in this Sector were 118 killed and 113 wounded, with 172 being captured. The casualties suffered by 4 Dogra were 110, while 4 Sikh had 180 casualties. The total casualties sustained by 11 Infantry Brigade during the battle of Walong were 340 killed 260 wounded and 332 captured.

## 11 Infantry Brigade Signal Section in Walong

11 Infantry Brigade was on its way from Kangpokpi in Naga Hills to Darranga near Bhutan when it was diverted to Chabua from where it was airlifted to Walong. The Section was then under the command of Captain Lal Singh. The Brigade Commander and his rover detachment which had already reached Darranga were flown to Chabua and then to Walong on 31 October 1962. The Brigade Headquarters and Signal Section reached Chabua by train and road on 1 November. Two

wireless detachments were immediately sent to Walong to work on D1 and B1 links, while the rest of the personnel and equipment moved by air over the next two days, when airlift became available. The vehicles and heavy equipment were left behind at Chabua. Since the battalions already had their wireless detachments with them, the Signal Section was asked to leave an equivalent number of personnel and equipment behind.

On arrival at Walong the Signal Section got down to the establishing the essential communications on line and radio with the battalions and rearwards. The lines to 4 Sikh and 3/3 Gorkha Rifles which were both located nearby were completed the same day, while the line to 6 Kumaon at Tri-Junction took more than two days. After the direct lines had been completed, lateral lines were laid between battalions. Multiple strands of cable were laid along steel twines across the Lohit River to ensure reliability. To improve survivability of local lines, these were laid through communication trenches on the side walls. Lines to the operations room and the Brigade Commander were duplicated, using different routes.

The line to Tri-Junction required considerable effort. The distance involved was about 15 miles from Walong (height 5000 feet) to Tri-Junction (height 13000 feet). The cable used was D8 (T), all on man pack. Speed being of the utmost importance, the route was divided into three sections. The cable was air dropped on drums No 5 Mk I, which were collected and placed at intervals of about half a mile with the help of porters and pioneers. Each section was laid by a different line party, working simultaneously. The route was completed in a very short time and worked well thereafter. Lance/Naik K. C. Singh, who was in charge of the line party working on the farthest section did a creditable job but was taken prisoner. The laying of the line was supervised by Jemadar Risal Singh, the Jemadar GD (general duties) of the Section. Though he was an operator by trade, he guided the linemen well.

All line laying was done on man pack basis. There were only six linemen, so each line party comprised just two linemen. One lineman was on duty on local lines and one was engaged on repair of faulty trunk lines. At times linemen were helped by operators for specific short durations. The lateral lines proved to be extremely useful and there was never a chance when at least one of the alternate lines to a battalion was not through. The Divisional Commander, General Pathania, who was in Walong on Night 15/16 November, remarked that he could speak to any platoon on telephone. The line to Tri Junction served another useful purpose – it served as a track guide to the troops being inducted into the area.

The wireless links to HQ 2 Infantry Division at Dinjan, D1 and D2, were based on 19 HP sets, using end fed wire aerials. For the B1 net to battalions, 62 sets were used, with rod aerials. The B21 net worked with the rear headquarters of the brigade at Chabua and the airfield at Tezu, using WS 19. The B1 net to battalions was not used except during attack for a short time and during withdrawal. The wireless links functioned well, though the speech was not clear during night on D1 when key conversations had to be resorted to. There was no interference experienced from the Chinese stations, though the detachment of the wireless experimental unit in Walong did monitor some messages of the Chinese. Captain Lal Singh recalls that he was once given a report about "a Chinese lady" passing a message on channel 8 of WS 31. He immediately opened the set and tried to monitor the channel but found nothing.

A major problem was man packing of WS No 62 with the 300 watt charging engine on the hills. The 80 watt engine did not function due to the low temperatures at heights. During the withdrawal two detachments with WS No 62 and charging set 300 watt engine were brought till the first halt. The charging set had to be abandoned thereafter. The rest of the equipment consisting of WS No 19/19 HP and 1260 watt engines had to be left since it could not be carried on man pack on the 110 mile long route, along with other essential stores. However, two wireless sets 31 were brought back by the Signal Section.

Wireless communication during withdrawal was not very satisfactory for several reasons. The entire route followed the valley, the track being hardly 1-2 ft. wide. Halts were dictated by the enemy at awkward places on narrow tracks on sheer rocks where there was hardly any place for correct direction and height of aerials. The halts were mostly during night between 11 pm and 4 am. The maintenance of the column had been planned but could not be carried out as one of the helicopters which came to deliver food to the battalion in a delaying position was shot down by the Chinese.

The SDS (scheduled despatch service) proved very useful. An ADS (air despatch service) was maintained between Chabua and Tezu using IAF Dakotas. At Chabua, a detachment of divisional signals was stationed to handle the SDS mail. At Tezu the Brigade Transport Officer, who was part of the B Echelon, was responsible for dispatch and receipt both ways. From Tezu an ADS was organised with IAF Otters for the maintenance of Walong garrison. At Walong airfield, a runner from the Brigade Signal Section collected the incoming mail and handed over the outgoing mail to the pilot. The battalions collected their mail by sending their runners to the signal centre every 3-4 hours. However, important messages with precedence 'Op Immediate' or above were cleared by a runner from the brigade. When the runner was not available, the battalion was informed on telephone to send their messenger.

11 Infantry Brigade Signal Section worked under trying conditions at Walong. The communications functioned well throughout, for which credit is due to the officer commanding, Captain Lal Singh. Though all ranks worked with dedication, the performance of Lance Naik Sat Parkash deserves special mention. He was the operator manning the wireless link with division. For his devotion to duty in maintaining communications on D2 net on 16 November 1962 under enemy shelling he was recommended for the award of VSM. In fact, four personnel (linemen and operators) were recommended for awards. Unfortunately, none of these came through. In the battle of Walong, 11 Infantry Brigade Signal Section had one officer, to JCOs and 62 OR. Out of these four OR were killed and six were taken prisoner. All these belonged to battalion wireless detachments, rover and line detachment.

# CHAPTER 6

# SIGNALS IN NEFA

## IV Corps Signals

As is well known, IV Corps was created on 4 October 1962 and Lieutenant General B.M. Kaul appointed its first Commander. This was a unique case of a military formation being created for a commander, instead of a commander being found for a formation. One of the first officers to join the newly formed headquarters was the Chief Signal Officer, Brigadier P.S. Gill. Since he had recently moved from Shillong to Delhi after handing over charge of Chief Signal Officer of XXXIII Corps to Brigadier M.B. K. Nair, he was familiar with the area and its problems. The story of his appointment and subsequent events are best described in his own words:-

> *"Biji's Kaul's IV Corps was born at midnight of 3rd Oct 62. I was awakened and summoned to Kaul's residence around 1 AM that night to be told by him personally, I had been selected to be his CSO. Lack of seniority, the basis of moving me from Shillong in May to Sigs Dte as DD Tels (the very job I had held as GSO1 Tels from 1953 to 1957) was given the go-by. Some 10 hours later (4th October) I accompanied him to Tezpur, in a Viscount of the Presidential flight. En route, quite naturally, I quizzed him regarding the role, area of responsibility of IV Corps and the troops allocation. He had no satisfactory answer*

*but kept on repeating "ap nahin samjhen ge." I was left with the impression that he was going to Tezpur more to instil some urgency into the Dhola affair/action.*

*I had never worked with Kaul. I was picked because I had known the NEFA region as CSO XXXIII Corps, since handed over to MBK Nair. Kaul left for LUMPU etc. on fifth. I was to organize and set up the new Corps HQ. Kaul had asked me to send the BGS and the CE to join him at the front on arrival. My good friend "Bhaiya" Rajwade who had been CE XXXIII Corps along with me and was shunted to the CME, also for lack of seniority, was brought in on 6th October as the CE. KK Singh of the Armoured Corps another good friend joined on the seventh as BGS. Both were sent on to join Kaul.*

*I soon realized what a clout Kaul wielded. DG P&T Nanjappa of the ICS, would call me twice a day to ascertain what he could do for IV Corps and so also other worthies at Army HQ. In no time there were direct telephone and teleprinter lines connecting Tezpur to Delhi. Nanjappa also gave me (on attachment) a P&T Dept LO IK Gupta, a very capable and efficient officer. As for SDS, Indian Airlines instituted a daily Viscount flight Delhi-Tezpur- Delhi a sort of daily Air Courier. Delhi planners in their keenness to fulfil Kaul's bidding failed to instruct the Courier aircraft to make a stop at Lucknow i.e. Eastcom HQ which nominally was controlling IV Corps. I put this right in time.*

*In the fortnight prior to the Chinese attack of Twentieth October there was very little that IV Corps could do for 7 Bde. I visited Zimithang (TAC HQ 4 Div) and met Ram Singh who despite the various odds had the situation under control. I was certainly appalled by the difficult terrain conditions and the extremely precarious porter-based supply line forward to Namka Chu. Recovery of air dropped supplies was as low as 30 percent-most of it falling into deep ravines. Two-seater Bell helicopter, which could carry very little, was the only efficient means of getting around."*

## IV Corps Signal Regiment

Though the skeleton Corps HQ had been created, it took some time before it got its integral signal regiment. Formal orders for the raising of IV Corps Signal Regiment at Agra were issued by Army HQ on 10 October 1962. The first Commanding Officer, Lieutenant Colonel S.N. Mehta and the Second-in-Command, Major P.S. Gill reported on 24 October. Two days later, three more officers – Captain H.S. Goel and Lieutenants N.T. Singh and I.S. Jaswal - joined the unit, along with 36 Junior Commissioned Officers and Other Ranks. Within the next few days, several more personnel joined the unit. Among the officers were Major Channan Singh (Officer Commanding 1 Company); Major Ranjit Singh (Quartermaster); Major H.V. Dixit (Technical Officer Telecom); Captain Y.P. Mittoo (Adjutant) and Captain S.R. Sharma (Cipher Officer).

On 10 November 1962, the advance party of the unit comprising one Junior Commissioned Officer and 39 Other Ranks left by rail for Tezpur under Lieutenant N.T. Singh. A day later a smaller party of ten men under Major H.V. Dixit left for Tezpur by air. The Commanding Officer left by air on 14 November, via Delhi where he was called for discussions by Army HQ. On 19 November a large quantity of essential equipment was moved by air from Agra to Tezpur, along with the personnel required to man the signal centre, exchange and cipher office. However, even before the detachment could start functioning at the new location, on 20 November HQ IV Corps was asked to move from Tezpur to Gauhati. All personnel of the detachment at Tezpur left for Guwahati by road, leaving a small party of 15 men under Captain H.S. Goel to man the signal centre at Tezpur. These orders were cancelled the very next day, and on 21 November HQ IV Corps was asked to move back to Tezpur. The personnel of the detachment also returned to Tezpur.

Meanwhile a party of four officers, two Junior Commissioned Officers and 40 Other Ranks had moved by train from Agra 20 November 1962 with section stores. On 21 November when they were passing through Lucknow the Movement Control Officer informed them that their destination had been changed from Gauhati to Tezpur. Soon afterwards the Chinese declared a cease fire and the operations came to an end. However, the induction of the unit at Tezpur continued. On 30 November the complement at Tezpur changed its name from Detachment IV Corps Signal Regiment to IV Corps Signal Regiment, while the portion of the unit at Agra became Rear HQ IV Corps Signal Regiment.

On 1 December the orderly room staff arrived and the Regimental HQ became functional. Two days later, all the personnel of 4 Infantry Divisional Signal Regiment who had been assisting the unit since 28 October were relieved and personnel of IV Corps Signal Regiment began manning the signal centre and exchange on their own. The officers holding important appointments in the unit at this time were Lieutenant Colonel S.N. Mehta (Commanding Officer); Major P.S Gill (Second-in-Command); Captain Y.P. Mittoo (Adjutant); Major Ranjit Singh (Quarter Master); Major Channan Singh (1 Company); and Major H.P Bhardwaj (2 Company).

## 4 Infantry Divisional Signal Regiment

As mentioned earlier, 4 Infantry Divisional Signal Regiment virtually disintegrated right at the beginning of the Chinese invasion on 20 October 1962, with the Commanding Officer becoming a prisoner and the Second-in-Command being killed. With the defences being overrun or vacated in quick succession and the Chinese systematically cutting the telephone lines, the only means of communication left with the brigades and battalions was wireless. The rapid rate of withdrawal often resulted in loss of signal equipment that could not be replaced, with the consequent adverse effect on communications.

The survivors of 7 Infantry Brigade Signal Company withdrew from Namka Chu and initially headed for Ziminthang little knowing that the Divisional HQ was already on its way to Tawang. Eventually most of them made their way to Bhutan, with a few being killed or captured by the enemy. By 24 October 1962 the Divisional HQ was established at Dirang Dzong. After the capture of Tawang by the Chinese on 25 October and their advance up to Walong in the Infantry

Brigade Sector there was a long pause in the fighting. On 26 October 1962 Lieutenant Colonel G.S. Sodhi assumed command of 4 Infantry Divisional Signal Regiment. The task given to 4 Infantry Division now was the defence of the Se La – Dirang - Bomdi La area. By 9 November 1962 the Divisional Headquarters and Signal Regiment was deployed at Dirang Dzong, with 62, 65 and 48 Infantry Brigades being located Se La, Tawang and Bomdi La respectively.

In the second phase of the Chinese operations, the Walong front crumbled on the morning of 16 November and 11 Infantry Brigade was forced to withdraw. On 17 November the enemy isolated the Divisional HQ and the Signal Regiment by establishing a road block about a kilometre North of Bomdi La on the Bomdi La-Dirang Dzong road after by passing Se La. 62 Infantry Brigade was ordered to move back to Dirang Dzong. During the withdrawal one officer and 32 Other Ranks of 62 Brigade Signal Company were missing. The survivors of the Brigade on reaching Dirang Dzong found it under enemy occupation as the Divisional HQ had left for Bomdi La on hearing the news of Chinese occupation of Munna Camp. On their way to Bomdi La, the Divisional HQ learnt through a radio message about the fall of Bomdi La. The Divisional HQ and elements of the Divisional Signal Regiment dispersed and made their way to the plains. 65 Infantry Brigade also suffered a similar fate. 48 Infantry Brigade had been withdrawn to Rupa from where the Chinese evicted them on November 19 and they reached Chakku foothills on the subsequent morning.

Stragglers of 4 Infantry Divisional Signal Regiment continued to arrive at Misamari, Charduar, Bhairakund and Tezpur for many days. The bulk of the unit equipment and vehicles were destroyed or lost. The casualties suffered by the unit were three officers and 21 Others Ranks killed, while one officer and 29 Others Ranks had become prisoners of war. On 7 February, 1963, the unit was converted to 4 Mountain Divisional Signal Regiment and moved back to Ambala shortly afterwards

A conspicuous feature of the operations was the apparent breakdown of command and control and lack of coordination between various formation headquarters. There were many instances of information not reaching higher headquarters in time or orders not being passed down the chain of command. This led to doubts on the reliability of communications provided by Signals. While it is true that communications did break down at certain periods, a detailed analysis reveals that most of the criticism is unfounded. Apart from the obvious constraints of lack of equipment and terrain, the systematic disruption of lines by the Chinese ensured that the only means of communications available once the operations commenced was wireless. The shortage of equipment, especially batteries and the electrolyte needed to keep them charged has been well documented. Another factor that needs to be kept in mind is that this was the first time Indian troops were operating in such terrain with almost total dependence on air supply for replenishment of essential spares and supplies including fuel, oil and lubricants. The fact that the Commander Signals of the Division had to personally carry a jar of sulphuric acid needed to charge the batteries of 7 Infantry Brigade Signal Company in Namka Chu shows the peculiar constraints under which the unit was working.

An important point that needs to be brought out is that most of the criticism about failure of communications originates from lack of authentic information and is based more on surmise than actual facts. Significantly, the formation commanders themselves have generally been appreciative of the quality of communication support provided to them by their signal units. In some cases, communications functioned until the last moment and ceased only when the headquarters itself closed down or withdrew, sometimes without informing the higher headquarters. There are several entries in war diaries of the formations and units that mention their inability to pass an important message or obtain the latest information because of lack of response from the other end. This naturally led to the conclusion that communications have broken down, a not uncommon occurrence in those days, given the type of equipment then in use.

The two signal officers who were primarily responsible for the communications during the critical phases of the operation were

Lieutenant Colonel K.K. Tewari, commanding 4 Infantry Divisional Signal Regiment and Captain Lakshman Singh, commanding 7 Infantry Brigade Signal Company. Both have dwelt on this aspect in their books as well as in inputs sought from them subsequently. Lieutenant Colonel K.K. Tewari writes:-

> *It has been said earlier that when something went wrong in operations there was a tendency to put the blame on Signals for the lack of communications. I had personal experience of this on many occasions before and after the 1962 operations. But in this particular case, although the staff did indulge in the same tactic, I am happy to note that the two commanders most intimately concerned with the battles in October have given a very balanced and correct picture about the signal communications in the books they wrote afterwards.*
>
> *Reference can be made to the books written by the GOC 4 Infantry Division, Maj Gen Niranjan Prasad and the Commander, 7 Infantry Brigade, the late Brig John Dalvi. I am grateful to them for having put the record right for the same of posterity and it would not be out of place in this narrative to quote from their books.*
>
> *Maj Gen Niranjan Prasad in his book, "The Fall of Towang" has this to say:*
>
> *"In order to ensure that I could influence the matters after battle has been engaged, it was imperative that I had good communications to all the sectors and posts concerned. In this, I had been served very well, both by my Chief Signals officer (Lt Col Tewari, even now on a visit to the Namka Chu area) and by his No 2, Maj Ram Singh, who was with me in Zimithang. My communication state, briefly, was as follows:-*
>
> *To the Rear – both line and wireless link with Corps HQ and my Rear HQ at Tezpur.*
>
> *To 7 Brigade Sector - line and wireless to all posts – but I could listen into all the wireless sets with units forward of Brigade – Tsangle, Tsang Dhar, Bridge 3 & 4 and 1/9 Gorkhas.*

*To Centre Sector – line and wireless to all posts – Bridge 1 & 2, Lumpu, Hathungla, Khinzemani, Chutangmu and Brokenthang.*

*To Towang Sector – line and wireless.*

*"My signals officers and personnel had ensured that the wireless sets and telephones worked well and I had no trouble in keeping touch with all the sectors and out posts. I was therefore confident of being able to help and guide my command once the attack had started .... The signallers manned their sets or telephones and coolly handled incoming and outgoing signals traffic".*

*That is from the Divisional Commander's book. As stated earlier, I was talking on the wireless set of the Gorkhas, first to the brigade HQ and then to the Divisional Tactical HQ, when the post was vacated by our troops and the two signalmen and myself were left behind.*

*Now to quote from Brig Dalvi's book "The Himalayan Blunder":*

*"On 11 September, I was constantly prodded to give the 'exact' location of the Assam Rifles and Punjab patrols which were moving post – haste to Dhola. My staff maintained round the clock vigil by the wireless set but could not establish contact. There were cynical and sarcastic remarks about the standard of 7 Brigade's wireless proficiency, as if the brigade signallers could redress the inadequacies of our antiquated equipment.*

*"On the evening of the 18th (October), Lt Col K.K. Tewari, Commander Signals of 4 Division arrived at my HQ .... He was able to brief me on what was going on at the Divisional HQ ... Col Tewari was a gentle God-fearing man in addition to being a first rate signaller. He had worked against tremendous odds throughout the operations and had overcome difficulties which would have taxed an Army Signals Regiment. He is due much credit for providing communications with obsolete equipment and the distances involved. Instead of praise they came in for criticism for not being able to work miracles with outdated sets and distances which were beyond the range of divisional signals.*

*"I was once asked to sack my Brigade Signals Officer but I refused and said I would prefer to be sacked myself. I was responsible for giving him*

*tasks which were beyond his capability. Tewari was grateful for my intervention on behalf of an innocent young officer. I hope that young Lachman Singh reads this small tribute from a grateful commander, for his untiring efforts to keep me in touch.*

*"There was a sad sequel to Tewari's visit. He asked my permission to visit 1/9 Gorkhas and I readily agreed. When the Gorkhas were attacked, Tewari found himself in the midst of an infantry battle. He was taken prisoner after the Chinese had overrun the position. Who has ever heard of a Commander Signals being sent to an infantry battalion on the night before a massive attack? He would have been at Divisional HQ attending to Division's requirements".*

Many years later, Major General K.K. Tewari was interviewed and his impressions recorded on tape. He was also given a questionnaire dealing with various events of that momentous period. In response to a specific question regarding failure of communications, he said:-

*Lot of incorrect statements have appeared in books and other articles written on 1962 ops, regarding failure of signal communications. Major Johri in his book "Chinese Invasion of NEFA" talks of only an Artillery set providing the only communications from 7 Infantry Brigade to the outside world on 20 October. This is absolutely false. There was no rear link of Artillery from Namka Chu area. Up to the time when the Chinese attack came on 20 October morning, both line and radio communications at HQ 7 Infantry Brigade forward as well as rearwards were fully operational and working entirely satisfactorily. Lines were systematically cut by the Chinese early that morning. This included the line to the DZ at Tsangdhar prior to the commencement of attack which was preceded by a heavy barrage of artillery and mortar fire. I spent the night of 19/20 October with 1/9 GR and was sitting on the rear link (B1) radio set talking to Brigadier Dalvi when the assault on the battalion HQ came and gave him a sort of running commentary on the battle. I later flicked the frequency to talk to Divisional HQ at Zimithang and spoke to my 2IC, the late Major Ram Singh. Rear link radio set of 2 Rajput was destroyed when it received a direct hit on the bunker, killing its occupants including the Mortar officer Captain Mangat and wounding the CO, Lieutenant Colonel (later Brigadier) Rikh seriously. As far as I know, 9 Punjab rear link radio set was working up to the time perhaps when the control set at brigade HQ packed up to withdraw. I am not sure of 4 Grenadiers rear link set.*

*On my return from China in May 1963. I was questioned by the SO-in-C Lieutenant General R.N. Batra about the communications and he wanted to know why the communications had broken down. I had to correct him with a firm remark which I remember distinctly: "communications were provided as long as the commanders and users were there to use them". This is a factual and true statement because I was left in the bunker with the rear link radio detachment talking as given above when the battalion HQ elements of 1/9 GR had withdrawn.*

*In fact the only people left behind were myself with two Signalmen (radio operators) and the RMO (Regimental Medical Officer), Captain Sud with his wounded in the RAP (Regimental Aid Post) and we were both taken prisoners of war in the battalion HQ area. Rest of the personnel of battalion HQ of 1/9 GR were captured later at other places while retreating and NOT in the battalion HQ area. It is interesting to note on Page 357 of Neville Maxwell's book 'India's China War' where he writes: "Dalvi, whose HQ was in the valley with his troops, asked Prasad for permission to withdrew, he remained in contact with 4 Division".*

*Communications were disrupted only when he Chinese attacked the rear link radio bunker in which I was sitting on the set with two of my signal operators. I fired with my 9mm Browning pistol and killed one Chinese and wounded another before the Chinese assaulted the bunker. The radio set was riddled with bullets, one of the radio ops killed outright and the other badly wounded.*

Captain Lakshman Singh has also quoted the remarks of Major General Niranjan Prasad and Brigadier Dalvi mentioned above. In addition, he writes:-

*Many commanders and staff officers have blamed communications for their failures in Training Exercises and in Operations. Brigadier PS Gill the then CSO 4 Corps had written in a letter to me, dated 30th January 2002, about his own experience. I quote. – "It is also my (1962) experience that often good signal communications, for some, was unmitigated nuisance since the user commander could be asked for decision or such like. So he was always 'gone forward' without the rover set. I once even asked one such commander as to where was his Rover WS. He replied he did not need one" – Unquote. Possibly this was also the reason that Lt Col Mishra CO 9 Punjab had left the Signals detachment on the Brigade net, as recorded earlier, behind at Lumla. I have already narrated the incident of my sacking. ........*

*My own commander, Brig Dalvi had his own views of Signals and I quote from his Book, "The Himalayan Blunder". Quote: "When the GOC ordered me to leave at once, I decided that someone had taken leave of his senses, so I pretended that I could not hear him and could not follow his orders due to heavy atmospherics. I asked the operator to tell the GOC to call me again when reception conditions improved ....." Unquote.*

*When informed by the operator of D1 of this and not being aware of the reason behind the instructions to the operator, I was most upset. Since with the 400 watt Transmitter at my disposal, I was confident and proud of providing communications round the clock, I was also aware of the quality of Radio link at that time. I do not remember as to how I reacted, did I speak to the BM or the Commander?*

*Brigadier Dalvi continues: "Again ..... 4 Division's Signals Regiment managed to get a telephone line through from Division to 7 Brigade over the Hatungla Pass. The line ran parallel to the Chinese forward defended positions for over seven miles, in violation of every principle of laying a line in the battle zone. The line was useful for conducting all the futile conversations that preceded the Chinese attack, but served no purpose whatsoever after the assault, as it was inevitably cut. This was one more feverish military activity under Chinese observation to give the illusion of feverish military preparations ......*

*........On 16 October I was able to set up my HQ at Rongla about 1000 yards from Dhola post. The location was not ideal but only one possible in the circumstances, unless I went to Tsangdhar.*

*Who knows, possibly we would all have been killed or taken prisoners, on 20th October, by the Chinese at Tsangdhar if the HQ had been set up there. But, this new location was the beginning of all my troubles in so far as communications go. It was totally unsuitable for wireless communications, heavy screening by thick vegetation and overhead cover of thick jungle trees, it was also sited deep in the valley of the River Namka Chu, with massive mountain features between the Brigade HQ and the Division TAC HQ at Ziminthang. In one stroke I had lost the advantage of the heights provided by Tsangdhar. All the signal officers of the battalions had been called to the Brigade HQ on 18th October for tying up the communications as we were having difficulty in contacting 9 Punjab and 4 Grenadiers, mainly due to siting of the sets and the terrain. The Signals detachments of these two battalions were still on move, these had been left behind of Lumpu for reasons best known to them, and they had opened there own sets on B1.*

In his letter of 30 January 2002 to Lakshman Singh mentioned above, Brigadier PS Gill goes on to record:-

*Those days I personally (from Tezpur) closed down the VHF (AN/TRC) link at Sela, as everyone of any consequence had vanished. The same happened at Darrang (4 Div HQ) and Bomdila (48 Bde HQ). Sodhi (who had taken KK's place) contacted me to know what he should do now that Anant Pathania and his GSO1 Manohar were nowhere to be seen. I authorised him to make his own way as best as practical. Lakhanpal, the 48 Bde Signals Officer, contacted me and presented a similar situation and I had to authorise the 'pull-out' and a move back by certain 'bounds'. He was intercepted by the Chinese at the second bound and was obliged to hide till nightfall in a nearby stream. A week later he turned up looking famished and underweight, but in good heart.*

*At the HB Committee later on, of course Signals were the favourite whipping boy. I however had taken good care, to provided convincing proof to the contrary in every case. Even our DD Sigs (Chakerbuti) had turned up at Tezpur 'to know what went wrong'. I directed him to the BGS who directed him back to me, saying 'nothing went wrong, and, to remember PS Gill gave us signal comns while we were retreating.*

## Signal Task Force (Project Tusker)

Two Signal Task Forces were raised at the General Reserve Engineering Forces (GREF) Centre at Allahabad in 1961. One Task Force was later sent to provide communications support to Project Beacon in Jammu and Kashmir, under the command of Lieutenant Colonel S.N. Atal. The second Task Force was raised by Lieutenant Colonel B.S. Panwar for Project Tusker in NEFA. After raising the Force, Colonel Panwar took the Force to the Foothills at Misamari. Prior to raising this Task Force, he had carried out extensive reconnaissance of the area that the Force was to operate in. The Task Force consisted of three companies. One company comprised personnel from the Corps of Signals. The other two companies comprised personnel from the GREF. The Task Force reached Tezpur on the 51st anniversary of the Corps i.e., on 15 February 1962.

The priority task assigned to the Force after arriving in NEFA was to construct two permanent line routes viz. North Lakhimpur – Lakhabali – Along and Tezpur – Misamari (Foothills) – Dirang Dzong – Bomdila – Tawang. Both routes were to be built up on 300 pounds copper wire. To start with only one pair was to be built on each of the two routes. One of the routes had reached just short of Bomdila when in September 1962, the Chinese started infiltrating across the border. After the infiltration commenced, Colonel Panwar ensured that only regular Army personnel were used for the construction ahead of Bomdila whereas GREF personnel were used for construction work in the rear, well away from the border. The Task Force was under the command of 4 Infantry Division.

When the induction of troops into the Namka Chu started, the Task Force provided assistance by making available all the transport which it had. The transport fleet with the Task Force -Nissan vehicles - was better than that with the Division which largely held the Second World War vintage 15 cwt. trucks. When it became clear that the Chinese meant business, Colonel Panwar speeded up the construction of the route Bomdila – Dirang Dzong – Sela – Tawang. Colonel Panwar managed to obtain some radio sets AN/TRC with which he established a radio relay link from Bomdila to Sela to provide a duplex speech circuit. After the initial attack on 20 October 1962, there was a lull in the battle that lasted almost a month. When the next major action took place on 17 November, Colonel Panwar was watching a film in the Officers Mess. His Adjutant, Captain S.V.S. Chaudhary, quietly walked up to him and told him that both Bomdila and Dirang Dzong were cut off. Colonel Panwar immediately spoke to the Brigadier General Staff at HQ IV Corps and came to know that the Chinese had once again infiltrated and cut off the lines.

Next day, on 18 November, Bomdila fell. Colonel Panwar spoke to Lieutenant Colonel G.S. Sodhi, who had taken command of the 4 Infantry Divisional Signal Regiment after the capture of Lieutenant Colonel K.K. Tewari. Colonel Sodhi informed him that they were abandoning Bomdila within the next hour. Six personnel of the Corps of Signals who were part of the Task Force and were involved in the maintenance of the lines ahead of Bomdila were killed. On 20 November the Chinese declared a unilateral cease fire. Later it was discovered that almost the entire route built up by the Task Force had been stripped of the copper wire. The Chinese had probably taken away all the copper.

# CHAPTER 7

# LADAKH

## Daulet Beg Oldi

Daulat Beg Oldi abbreviated as DBO, was an important post in Ladakh on the Old Silk Route, which led to Yarkand in Sinkiang. The position was held by 14 Jammu & Kashmir Militia and a company of 5 Jat. Following the pattern of the deployment dictated by the 'Forward Policy', only the Battalion HQ and a company were located in DBO, the rest distributed in 21 small posts covering various approaches. Ten posts were located in the Chip Chap river valley, while four were guarding the approach from another river to the south. In addition there were a few troops' staging posts on the line of communication from Leh. The principal means of replenishment was by airdrops and a few available MI 4 helicopters. All the posts were equipped only with small arms with the exception of one that had a section of 3-inch mortars. The distance between the posts ranged from 2 to 12 km, and none were mutually supporting. Their capability to defend themselves or with Chinese incursions movement was inadequate.

The Chinese had been building up their strength in the sector from July 1962 onwards, unhindered due to own lack of resources and the policy of not provoking the Chinese. Shortly before the invasion, on 19 October 1962, the Chinese had surrounded or dominated all the Indian posts in Chip Chap valley. The Chinese started their offensive on 19 October 1962 with simultaneous attack on two Indian posts, one held by a section of 14 J&K Militia and the other by a few men of 5 Jat. The Chinese used more than a company supported by mortars and medium machine guns against each post, whose defences consisted of open trenches and *sangars* (stones placed in a heap above ground level). The posts fought back and withstood the Chinese onslaught until next morning when they went out of communications with the Headquarters, this being the first indication that they had been overrun.

In the early hours of the morning on 20 October, the Chinese launched attacks on two other posts on the northern bank of Chip Chap River, held by 5 Jat, whose personnel were asked to fall back on another post. This resulted in the isolation of another post called Chandni held by a platoon of 14 J&K Militia, located on high ground. After one hour of shelling, at 6 am on 20 October the Chinese attacked the post, which could not be reinforced since the route had been blocked by the enemy. After beating back three attacks the post fell. Similar attacks were launched on other posts during the day, but by the end of 20 October, the Chinese had succeeded in capturing four posts, the others still holding out. Information regarding these events was conveyed on wireless by DBO Headquarters to HQ 114 Brigade at Leh and through them to HQ XV Corps at Udhampur. Appreciating that the Chinese would soon cut the line of communication, HQ 114 Brigade recommended to HQ XV Corps that isolated posts should be asked to pull back and concentrate at DBO.

During the night of 21 October, the remaining isolated posts were ordered to fall back on DBO, which was soon surrounded by the Chinese. On 22 October, the battalion commander sought the brigade commander's permission to withdraw the troops to a more defensible position. The Corps HQ was fully in picture and as early as 20 October itself had ordered 114 Brigade to withdraw the isolated posts. However, DBO, Post 14 (Jyotish), Track Junction, Sultan, Chushku, and Galwan Shyok river junction, which were tactically sound, were to be strengthened and held.

At 6 p.m. on 22 October 1962, HQ 114 Brigade asked 14 J&K Militia to commence withdrawal, which started at 9 pm. To deceive the enemy, who had been known to be intercepting our wireless nets, the Battalion Commander passed a false message to HQ 114 Brigade indicating that he had decided to hold on to DBO and Track Junction. The withdrawing troops destroyed all the heavy stores, including 3 inch mortars, recoilless guns and most wireless sets. The platoon of 1 Mahar refused to destroy their Vickers machine guns and carried them along. The seven available vehicles - mostly jeeps and a few 1 tons - were loaded with the sick and wounded and driven on the frozen river surface. However, about 24 km from DBO, the frozen surface gave way under the weight of the vehicles which had to be abandoned. It was an organized withdrawal, with the advance party led by Major Randhawa, who was familiar with the route and the main body under Lieutenant Colonel Nihal Singh. A rear party consisting of a platoon of J&K Militia under Captain S.P. Rigzin, occupied the dominating features of Pt. 18763, withdrawing only on 23 October to a half-way point. This marked the end of the fighting in Daulet Beg Oldi during the 1962 operations.

## Changchenmo and Galwan

The Galwan post was held by a company of 5 Jat, with the rest of the Battalion at Phobrang. The posts at Hot Spring, Nala Junction and Patrol Base were held by a platoon each, in addition to a post opposite the Chinese position at Tsogtsalu. In the first week of October, 5 Jat relieved 1/8 Gorkha Rifles, which had been holding the post earlier when it was in the news for not budging when surrounded by the Chinese in September. Coinciding with their attack elsewhere in the Ladakh, the Chinese launched an attack on Galwan post in the early hours of 20 October 1962. Communications with the post also ceased but sound of light machine gun and 2 inch mortar firing could be heard from the direction of the post. On 21 October Indian helicopters sent to fly over the area were fired at by the Chinese and no contact could be established with Galwan post. On his return the pilot reported that he saw no signs of life on the post. Details of the fighting at the Galwan post were known only after the return of Indian prisoners of war.

The Chinese attack on the post had started at 5.30 am on 20 October with heavy artillery and mortar bombardment, which destroyed most of the temporary shelters and tents. After an hour of shelling the Chinese attacked the forward sections with nearly a battalion. The defending troops moved to open trenches and fought a last ditch battle, with small arms, there being no artillery or mortars. After the forward positions had been overrun the rear positions continued to fight and it was only in the evening that the Chinese succeeded in capturing the post after launching their third attack. Out of 68 Indian personnel in Galwan, 36 were killed. The exact number of Chinese casualties is not known, but they were no doubt heavy, as can be deduced from the caution they displayed when tackling other posts such as Patrol Base, Nala Junction and Hot Spring. The Galwan post battle also demolished the assumption that was the foundation of the 'Forward Policy' viz. the Chinese back down if the defender stands his ground.

After eliminating the Indian posts in the Galwan valley, the Chinese turned their attention to Changchenmo valley in the south, which had platoon-sized posts at patrol Base, Nala Junction and Hot Spring, with the Company HQ at Hot Spring. On 21 October, the Chinese shelled all the three Indian posts. Since the utility of Patrol Base as a link between the Nala Junction and Galwan posts and had come to an end with the fall of the latter, it was ordered to withdraw to Nala Junction. As darkness fell, the platoon broke contact and withdrew, leaving behind a section to cover their move. Next morning, on 22 October, the Chinese launched an assault on this section. The men fought with great bravery and caused many casualties to the Chinese before being overwhelmed.

At 2 pm on 22 October 1962, the Chinese launched an attack on Kongma post on the southern flank which was held by a platoon 5 Jat, which fought for four hours before being overrun. Out of 33 men at Kongma only seven survived and withdrew to the Battalion base at Phobrang under the cover of darkness. The Chinese also attacked the platoon post at Anne La on the same day. The post fell by last light on 22 October after a stiff fight. With the fall of these two posts the Chinese were now in a position to pose a threat to the rear of the Indians deployed in Changchenmo valley.

The situation became critical, as from Kongma the Chinese could cut off the Jats deployed at Hot Spring, Nala Junction and Tsogatsalu. On 23 October HQ XV Corps issued orders to withdraw all troops and prepare positions at Tsogatsalu, Shortly afterwards, HQ 114 Brigade ordered even Tsogatsalu area to be abandoned and the troops to withdraw to Phobrang. Due to the extreme cold, nearly every one suffered from frost bite or chilblains during the withdrawal by a difficult route to Phobrang. The situation soon stabilized, and on 24 October a platoon under Major Ajit Singh of 5 Jat reoccupied Nala Junction. By 28 October, 5 Jat had consolidated their positions from Shyok to Phobrang. The forward positions at Tsogatsalu continued to be held and Indian patrols could still dominate the area. The Chinese did not attempt any further advances in this sector and situation remained unchanged right up to the ceasefire.

## Chushul

The defences of Chushul were held by two companies of 1/8 Gorkha Rifles, After being relieved by 5 Jat in second week of October 1962, a company less platoon strength was deployed in Sirijap complex North of Pangong lake. This post was supplied by boats across the lake and had no land link with the battalion. South of Pangong lake was the Yula complex comprising three posts manned by another company of 1/8 Gorkha Rifles. Nearly two companies defended the Spangur gap, holding the hill on the northern shoulder named Gurung hill and to the south named Nagar hill, in addition to a post in the gap itself.

Since early September the Chinese had surrounded the Sirijap post. The enemy strength opposite Chushul sector was estimated to be a regiment. At about 6 am on 21 October 1962 the Chinese commenced their assault on Sirijap after heavy shelling, using light tanks against which the defenders had no weapons. Soon after the shelling started communication with Sirijap was disrupted. A patrol from another post reached within 1000 yards of Sirijap-1 but could not see any signs of life on the post. On its return it reported that the entire post including the company commander Major Dhan Singh Thapa had been killed. After capturing Sirijap-1 the Chinese attacked and captured Sirijap-2 after heavy fighting. The few who escaped reported that after collecting the wounded the Chinese lined them up and shot them dead. By 22 October the Chinese were in complete control of the Northern bank of Pangong Lake.

On 21 October, a two mile long column of Chinese vehicles had been seen proceeding towards Spangur gap by Indian transport aircraft flying in the area. The move of Chinese vehicles was confirmed by troops in the area, causing alarm regarding imminent threat to Chushul. Since there was only a weak battalion covering the entire front of nearly 60 km from Changchenmo to Dungti, 13 Kumaon was ordered to move from Leh to Chushul. A platoon of 1 Mahar with medium machine guns and a field battery equipped with 25-pounders was also ordered to Chushul. However, the Chinese attack came only after the lull period was over.

## The Indus Valley

The Indus valley sector to the south of Chushul was held by 7 J&K Militia. The Battalion HQ with one company was in Koyul, a company was in Dungti and the rest of the troops deployed along the passes on the International border. The Chinese were estimated to have a battalion located in Tashigong. The Chinese attacks in this sector started on 27 October, with simultaneous assaults on Changla, Jarala, New Demchok and high ground (northwest of Demchok).

Changla was a well dug in post held by 17 men of 7 J&K Militia under a Junior Commissioned Officer. Early in the morning on 27 October, the Chinese opened fire on the Indian post with machine guns mounted on vehicles. The Indians returned the fire with 2-inch mortars, setting fire to the leading Chinese vehicles. As the enemy came closer, he was engaged with rifles and machine guns. After fighting resolutely for three hours, when he found himself surrounded by about 300 Chinese, the post commander decided to withdraw. Dividing his men in two parties, he ordered half of them to move while the other remained to give covering fire, he himself manning the light machine gun. Most of the men were able to withdraw to Fukche but the post commander was killed..

Jarala, which was held by 17 men under a Havildar, was attacked at the same time as Changla. About 200 Chinese surrounded the post from all sides and began firing with machine guns, the Indian replying with 2-inch mortars and light machine guns. After fighting through the day at last light the post commander decided to break out and re-join the battalion main defences at Koyul. Using fire and move the men successfully withdrew during the night.

In the south at New Demchok and High Ground the situation was different. High Ground was a well dug position held by five platoons, which had had two sections of 3-inch mortars and two medium machine guns. About 200 to 300 Chinese attacked the position in the early hours of 27 October. However, in the face of defensive fire of mortars and machine guns they had to beat a hasty retreat, after suffering heavy casualties. For the rest of the day, the Chinese were pinned down and could not move, since the ground was open. Unfortunately, the fall of Changla, Jarala and New Demchok cut the route of withdrawal as well as maintenance of the post, forcing it to pull out. Reluctantly, Battalion HQ ordered the post to withdraw at 7.30 pm on 27 October and the men were redeployed at Fukche.

It was in this battle that Signalman DC Dhilan was awarded a Vir Chakra. The citation of the award is given below:-

> *Sigmn (ORL) Dharam Chand Dhilan was in charge of the signal communication of a post in Damchok area in Ladakh, that was shelled and attacked by the Chinese on 27th October 1962. When a direct hit destroyed the wireless set, he took up a position in the trenches and fought until he was over powered by the Chinese. The devotion to duty and courage displayed by Sigmn Dharam Chand Dhilan were in the highest traditions of our Army and he was awarded the "Vir Chakra".*

New Demchok post across the Indus was a 'Forward Policy' post on the International border, not tactically sited. It was held by two platoons that were deployed in the historic Zorawar fort area. About 400 Chinese attacked the post in the morning on 27 October and suffered heavy casualties from the heavy fire from Zorawar fort. Some Chinese crossed the Indus and positioned themselves in the area of old Demchok on the western bank between High Ground and New Demchok, threatening the southern positions of 7 J&K Militia. The troops were ordered to withdraw in conjunction with those at High Ground during the night 27/28 October. The withdrawal was successfully completed and the men reached Koyul by 11.30 pm after evading a Chinese road-block under cover of darkness.

The newly established 3 Himalayan Division as well as HQ XV Corps considered a withdrawal from Koyul as well, but left the decision to the Commanding Officer, Lieutenant Colonel R.M. Banon. He preferred to stay put and strengthen the defences rather than withdraw. As a result, the Indians continued to occupy these positions. There was some confusion regarding outposts at Hanle, Zarser and Chumar which were held by CRP/ITBP and were not in communication after 27 October. These posts were also presumed to have fallen to the Chinese but it was learned on 31 October that they were all intact. When the fighting in this sector ended on 28 October, the Chinese had established control of the eastern hills flanking the Indus valley. They dominated the road that passed through the valley, denying its use by the Indians. The Chinese had apparently achieved their aim and there was no further fighting in this sector.

## The Lull: 28 October to 18 November

With the well co-coordinated Chinese attack in Ladakh and NEFA on 20 October 1962, the basic hypothesis of the 'Forward policy' stood disproved. HQ Western Command, which had been pleading for deployment based on military logic considerations rather than guess work, felt itself vindicated and now put into action its own plan for defence of Ladakh. The earlier operating injunction about not withdrawing resources and troops facing Pakistan was revoked and between 20 October and 30 October, nearly a division worth of troops was inducted in Ladakh. To achieve this task, ad hoc measures were taken on a war footing. To offset the severe shortage of transport, the first line transport from units and formations was withdrawn to form ad hoc transport companies to help the induction process. Battalions were taken from divisions facing Pakistan, after evaluation of the threat in each sector. The transport fleet of the Indian Air Force was utilized much beyond its normal capacity. Most of the inducted troops were earmarked for the defence of Leh, the strength in the forward most posts being augmented only marginally.

Many new formations and units were raised to control the large number of troops deployed in the sector. On 26 October 1962 Major General Budh Singh, MC raised 3 Himalayan Division at Leh. HQ 114 Brigade was moved to Chushul and made responsible for Chushul and Phobrang sectors. Brigadier R.S. Grewal, MC, arrived in Leh with HQ 70 Infantry Brigade on 25 October and took over responsibility of the Indus Valley sector. By 3 November it was established at Dungti and later at Asle in the rear. On 24 October Delta sector was raised out of existing troops to look after the Northern sector, with its Headquarters at Thoise. HQ 163 Infantry Brigade arrived in Leh to look after the close defence of the town itself. Since 114 Brigade, which was directly under HQ XV Corps, was bearing the brunt of the fighting, the existing structures were left intact and HQ 3 Division interfered very little in its functioning. Additional infantry battalions were also inducted. These included 9 Dogra, 3/4 Gorkha Rifles, 3 Sikh Light Infantry and 1 Jat. The troops were airlifted in small groups and deployed to plug the gaps in the defences. In view of the likelihood of the road to Chushul being cut off, the Corps of Engineers were asked to construct an alternative route via Karu, Changla, Tangtse and Tartar Camp.

To enhance the fire power of troops in Ladakh, 13 Field Regiment equipped with 25-pounder field guns was inducted. One battery of this unit was already in Chushul. By 3 November another battery reached Dungti. The third battery was located in Leh along with the Regimental Headquarters. 114 Heavy Mortar Battery equipped with 4.2 inch mortars was inducted in Chushul between 26 October and 31 October. One troop was sent to Lukung to support 5 Jat and the rest of the battery was sent to Dungti. The Indian Air Force achieved a major feat when the AN-12 aircraft airlifted a troop of AMX-13 tanks of 20 Lancers to Chushul on 25 October 1962.

On 30 October HQ XV Corps informed HQ Western Command that 3 Himalayan Division was not being asked to make any plan for withdrawal from Chushul, as it was felt that this would have an adverse effect on the morale of the troops who had given a good account of themselves in the recent battles with the Chinese. Orders were issued that Chushul and Dungti were to be defended to the last man. A bid was also made for close air support to support the defensive battle.

All possible routes to Leh were held in strength. In the north, D Sector with strength of nearly two battalions held the Saserla, Sultan Chushku, Shyok, and Galwan-Shyok river junction. The route passing over Changla was defended at the pass itself, as well as at Dorbuk. To give depth to the Changla defences, troops were deployed at Phobrang and Chushul with some artillery support. In the Indus Valley sector, a whole brigade blocked the axis at Dungti, Chumathang and areas further back. In Leh proper there was nearly a battalion worth of troops to defend the surrounding hills. The newly inducted troops were well placed to defend Leh. Only one battalion, 1 Jat, was deployed in Chushul area. Commander 114 Brigade made a bid for additional troops for the defence of Chushul, but this was turned down by the Corps Commander, who had decided that priority must be given to the defence of Leh.

## Battles of Rezangla and Gurung Hill

The Chinese utilized the lull period to build up their strength in the Spangur area. This was not hidden from Indian troops occupying Gurung hill and Yula III, who duly reported these activities. In the absence of long range weapons and decision not to use Air Force, the Indians did not have the capability to interfere with the Chinese build up, which continued unabated. Indian build up was proceeding apace but it had been decided not to send the newly inducted troops to threatened areas like Chushul.

After the raising of 3 Himalayan Division, 114 Brigade moved to Chushul on 27 October and assumed sole responsibility for the defence of this sector. Out of the three battalions that were part of the Brigade, 1 Jat had a company each at Tokung, Yula III and Lukung while the rest of the battalion was at Gompa Hill. 1/8 GR was deployed to cover the Northern flank of Spangur gap, with two companies on Gurung hill and a company to the North of Pt. 5167. The fourth company was located in the Spangur gap itself, while the battalion headquarters was located at the airfield with an ad hoc company as reserve. 13 Kumaon was looking after the Southern flank with two companies on Muggar Hill, a company with section of 3 inch mortars at Rezangla and battalion headquarters with one company at Track Junction. Tsakla also had a company of 5 Jat. The total frontage held by the brigade was nearly 40 Km. Most of the troops were committed to ground holding role and the only reserves available at the brigade level were two troops of tanks and an ad hoc company located at the airfield.

The Chinese had concentrated nearly a regiment plus a battalion in the vicinity of the Spangur gap. The two major concentrations were in area North of Gurung hill and in Spangur gap itself. They had deployed their heavy mortars in the gap in full view of the Indians deployed on Gurung hill. On 29 October the Chinese opened mortar fire on Gurung hill. Once the Indian guns opened up and engaged the Chinese Observation Post located at Black Top, that overlooked Gurung hill, the Chinese promptly stopped their fire.

The real Chinese attack in this sector started on 18 November, coinciding with their attack on Se La in NEFA. In a co-coordinated attack on Chushul defences the Chinese used nearly two battalions in south against Rezangla and about a regiment in the north. Rezangla is an isolated 18000 ft high feature, about 11 km south of Spangur gap. The importance of Rezangla was that it dominated the road link with Leh that went via Dungti, which was the life line of the Chushul garrison. The nearest Indian position to the south was 5 Jat Company at Tsakla. The Rezangla position, though forming part of the main defences, was thus in reality an isolated company post. The battery of 13 Field Regiment located in Spangur gap could not support Rezangla, which only had the section of 3-inch mortars located within the company position as fire support. In view of its isolated location, the company was sited for all round defence.

Early in the morning on 18 November, the forward observation post to the south of company defences detected nearly 400 Chinese approaching the defences. The company immediately went to their trenches but held their fire waiting for the Chinese to come within range. Soon, nearly a battalion of the enemy assaulted Rezangla from the south and the east. At about 5 am, when the enemy had climbed up the slopes and was within range, the Kumaonis opened fire. Caught in the deep nullahs, the Chinese suffered heavy casualties from 3-inch mortars and grenades. After nearly half an hour of intense fighting the attack lost momentum, the assaulting Chinese taking shelter behind boulders.

Once the Chinese failed to capture the position by a silent attack, they opened artillery and mortar fire. Though the fire was not very effective and did not cause much damage to the defences, the telephone lines to the Battalion HQ were cut and the radio set destroyed. C Company of 13 Kumaon was now out of touch with the rest of the battalion. The post at Tsakala could see the firing and reported the news of the fight to the Battalion HQ. Under the cover of artillery fire, the Chinese in two company strength attacked the rear platoon. The Indians jumped out of their trenches and tackled the enemy with bayonets and even bare bands. All the men of this platoon died fighting, and there was not a single survivor. However, the 3-inch mortars were continuously firing at the advancing enemy at point blank range and the ground was littered with Chinese dead. The Company Commander, Major Shaitan Singh, moved from trench to trench, encouraging his men and redeploying the light machine guns. He was ably assisted by his Havildar Major, who was always at his side and with fixed bayonet warded off many attacks on the Company Commander, sending many Chinese soldiers to their graves.

Rezangla was a hard fought battle. The Indian machine gun fell silent only at about 10 pm. The ferocity of the of fighting can be gauged from the fact that, out of 112 all ranks at Rezangla, only 14 survived and no prisoners were taken by the Chinese. In November 1963, nearly a year after the battle, the dead bodies were recovered by the Indian Red Cross. The parties that visited Rezangla saw the place littered with field dressings and blood marks, giving some idea of the heavy losses suffered by the Chinese. The Company Commander, Major Shaitan Singh, was awarded the Param Vir Chakra for the battle of Rezangla.

The Chinese attacked Gurung hill complex simultaneously with their attack on Rezangla. At 5.30 am on 18 November, the Chinese began intense bombardment of Gurung hill as well as the Indian posts located in the Spangur gap and Muggar Hill. Two companies of 1/8 Gorkha Rifles were defending the East area of Gurung Hill. The first wave of the attackers made contact with the northern company on Gurung hill at 6.30 am. When still outside small arms range, they were engaged by accurate fire from the troop of 13 Field Regiment. The enemy launched a series of attacks and after two hours succeeded in occupying some portions of Gurung hill. The Gorkhas came out of their trenches and fell on them with their *khukris* (a small curved knife). Unable to face this fierce onslaught, the Chinese fell back. By 10 am the situation became stable and Gurung hill remained firmly in Indian hands.

The Chinese soon launched another attack, which was preceded by intense shelling. The brave Gorkhas were finally overwhelmed by vastly superior numbers and the forward platoon fell. Out of 17 men in this platoon, not even one survived. The Chinese then turned their attention to the lower company. At this stage, they came under accurate fire from the tank troop of 20 Lancers. With no answer to the tanks, the Chinese suffered heavily and fell back.

The Gorkhas had suffered heavy casualties, with nearly 50 killed and several wounded. With the shelling of the airfield and village, reinforcements as well as ammunition supply was difficult. At this crucial juncture the line and radio communications link between Gurung hill and Battalion as well as Brigade HQ was disrupted due to heavy shelling. Keeping in mind the overall picture, HQ 114 Brigade decided to withdraw the troops from Gurung hill, Muggar hill, Spangur post and Tokung and to redeploy them on mountains west of Chushul. This was in conformity with instructions of HQ XV Corps, and the new positions had been already decided. The closing down of Chushul airfield and threat to Dungti track after fall of Rezangla meant that the brigade was now dependent on the long and difficult mule track from Leh that passed over the Changla and reached Chushul via Tangtse and Tartar camp. It was clear that while the defenders might be able to hold on for some more time, the sacrifice in men and material would not be justified. The Brigade Commander, Brigadier T.N. Raina, ordered a withdrawal on the night of 19/20 November.

The withdrawal was conducted in an orderly manner and most of the major equipment was retrieved. A major share of the credit for the successful withdrawal is due to the battery of 13 Field Regiment, which carried out accurate shelling of the Chinese positions during this period. On 19 November the Chinese launched another determined attack around mid-day on Gurung hill. But the artillery and tank fire was so accurate that the enemy had to fall back and made no further attempt. After the Indian troops had withdrawn the Chinese occupied Gurung hill. The Chinese did not follow up the withdrawing Indians. They also made no attempts to secure the Chushul airfield for their own use, as that would have meant tackling the Indian defences west of Chushul.

Chushul was the only organized defensive battle fought by the Indian Army in 1962. Though the Chinese outnumbered the Indians in numbers and had more fire support, the contest was close, and honours even. If 114 Brigade had an extra battalion and an artillery regiment, which is the normal fire support complement of a brigade, it is quite likely that they would have been able to repel the attacks on Gurung hill and Rezangla and win the battle of Chushul.

## 114 Infantry Brigade Signal Company in Ladakh

114 Infantry Brigade Signal Company was in Leh at the beginning of the year 1962. The company was then under the command of Major

P.K. Mukherjee with Captain P.C. Route as his second-in-command. As part of the Forward Policy a large number of posts were established in Chushul and the Indus valley region, by 1/8 Gorkha Rifles and 7 Jammu & Kashmir Militia. In the absence of Major Mukherji who was on leave, Captain Route, the officiating Company Commander was given the responsibility of coordinating the communication arrangements of the newly established posts. Setting out from Leh on 2 January by air for Adampur, Route was able to land at Fukche airfield only six days later on 8 January. Between 9 and 18 January, he visited the signal detachments of 7 Jammu & Kashmir Militia at Koyul, Fukche, New Demchok, High Ground, Dumchele, Dungti and Sakala. After visiting Rezangla on 19 January he proceeded to 1/8 Gorkha Rifles at Chushul and Phobrang. Soon after his return to Leh it was learned that Major P.K. Mukherji had been admitted to the Military Hospital in Allahabad and was unlikely to return. He was struck off strength on 30 January and Captain Route appointed Officer Commanding, with Lieutenant S.S. Sahney as the second-in-command.

Since 114 Brigade was directly under HQ XV Corps, technical control over the Signal Company was exercised by Chief Signal Officer XV Corps, Colonel Ajit Singh. To cater for the increased commitments of the Signal Company, it was given some additional equipment. In February 1962 it received one medium power radio set SCR 399 and two PE 95 generators from Chief Signal Officer XV Corps. A month later trials were carried out of radio set SCR 694 with hand generators GN 58, on Road Leh – Sheora at a distance of about 50 miles, climbing to a height of approximately 17000 ft. The communication on the link was found to be quite good. It was therefore decided to use the set with the Brigade Commander's Rover. In April 1962 Brigadier S.N. Gairola, who had taken over as the Chief Signal Officer XV Corps, visited Leh and discussed the communications problems with the Officer Commanding. Shortly after this, four miles of additional cable electric W110B (Single) was sent to Daulet Beg Oldi by helicopter along with two wireless sets 48 for providing wireless communications for patrols in the area. In May trials were carried out with radio set 76 and R209 on Road Leh – Rangbir Pura – Kaura at a distance of 15 miles.

By this time another officer, Lieutenant P.B. Vartak had also joined. In the middle of the year Major R.M. Rajan was posted in and assumed the appointment of Company Commander, Captain Route reverting to his original post of second-in-command. In view of the increase in commitments of 114 Infantry Brigade Signal Company, in September 1962 some changes were carried out in the existing communications set up. It was decided that T Communication Zone Signal Regiment would be responsible for the communications in Leh and rearwards, with 114 Infantry Brigade Signal Company being responsible only for communications forward of Leh. For this purpose, 2 Company of T Communication Zone Signal Regiment was asked to send 50 personnel to Leh, who would take over the signal centre and line communications at Leh. They would also operate and maintain the wireless links working back from Leh. However, overall responsibility for communications in Ladakh would remain with Officer Commanding 114 Infantry Brigade Signal Company, who would also provide additional manpower and equipment, if required, to augment the resources of T Communication Zone Signal Regiment deployed at Leh.

By 10 October 1962, the 50 men from T Communication Zone Signal Regiment had arrived at Leh and taken over the signal centre, local lines and rear wireless links. After the Chinese attacks on 20 October 1962 on Daulet Beg Oldi, Galwan and Changchenmo valley, events moved rapidly. It was decided to move HQ 11 Infantry Brigade to Chushul, with the newly raised 3 Himalayan Division being located at Leh. On 25 October Major Rajan was sent to carry out reconnaissance for a new location for the Brigade HQ on Axis Leh – Dungti. The Tactical Group of HQ 11 Infantry Brigade left Leh next morning at 4 am. It was accompanied by the advance party of the Signal Company under Captain Harbhajan Singh, who had reported arrival only two days earlier to relieve Captain Route, who went along with the party. They arrived at Chushul at 4 pm on 27 October after losing a lineman who died in a vehicle accident en route. By 28 October the advance party had set up skeleton communications at Chushul. The rest of the Signal Company under Major Rajan joined them on 30 October.

Brigadier S.N. Gairola, Chief Signal Officer XV Corps, visited Chushul on 7 November. He was accompanied by Lieutenant Colonel Harjit Singh, Commander Signals 3 Himalayan Division. By 10 November full scale line and wireless communications had been established to all posts and battalion headquarters and to Leh. The detachment of 2 Company T Communication Zone Signal Regiment in Chushul was relieved and de-inducted. Line communications between Chushul and Leh was provided by extending the existing permanent line at Shera to Chushul by ground PVC cable. This was done with the assistance of 11 Signal Company, Project Beacon.

On 16 November the Brigade Commander, Brigadier T.N. Raina, sent Major Rajan to Leh to bring up the remnants of the Brigade HQ and some additional signal equipment. Shortly afterwards, the Chinese attacked Rezangla and Gurung Hill. However, the communications remained stable and was commended by the Brigade Commander. Immediately after this it was decided to move the Brigade HQ to Tartar Camp. On 19 November a line was laid to the new location. On 27 November the advance party of the Brigade HQ and Signal Company moved to Thangse, with the main body arriving two days later. Communications at Chushul were handed over to a detachment of 2 Company T Communication Zone Signal Regiment. On 10 December, the Brigade HQ and Signal Company moved again, to Darbuk. By 12 December lines had been laid to all units of the Brigade in Darbuk. Rearward communication to Leh was established by a poled PVC route between Leh and Darbuk via Changla.

# CHAPTER 8

# REMINISCENCES

Some memories and experiences of signal officers who took part in the 1962 operations have been included in the relevant chapters of the book. As mentioned in the Preface, these include inputs from Brigadier PS Gill, Major General KK Tewari, Brigadier Lakshman Singh and Brigadier Lal Singh. However, in addition to these, there is a lot more, not all of which can be mentioned due to its sheer size or relevance. In addition, I have received inputs from several others who were then serving in units or formations other than 4 Infantry Divisional Signals Regiment and HQ IV Corps. Some of these are given in this chapter.

## Brig PS Gill - Notes on the NEFA (1962) Debacle.

Its 1360 km long mountainous frontier was being looked after by 4 Division less a brigade, and a few AR (Assam Rifles) posts which were withdrawn further back during winter months to avoid being cut-off (snowbound). Opportunity to settle Aksai Chin vs. McMahon line was lost already.

Nehru's reluctance to own up to Hindi-Chini Bhai-Bhai myth - a purely Nehruvian invention or (shall we say) an exercise in self-delusion. He even canvassed for a Security Council seat for the new Chinese Government. Why?

Biji Kaul was promoted Lt Gen in June 1959 against Thimmy's recommendation to the contrary since he found him unfit - so Army proceeded downhill. Thimmy resigned on 31 Aug 1959. He had advised all along – avoid confrontation with the Chinese - employ diplomacy instead. (*Author's Note - Thimayya had resigned on 31 Aug 1959 due to differences with the then Defence Minister, VK Krishna Menon. He later withdrew his resignation. He finally retired on 8 May 1961).*

XXXIII Corps under Lt Gen Umrao Singh was set up at Shillong mid - 1960, without much resources – more a parking place for newer promotees.

Embarked on the Forward Policy-Biji Kaul's brainchild- i.e. firm up on *what was thought to be the McMahon Line.* He believed 'Possession is Nine Tenth of the Law' and said so at every opportunity. AR posts were to remain forward for the winter months -supplied by Air? Immediate Chinese reaction was Khinzemane incident north of Towang.

Capt Mahabir of 1 SIKH sited Dhola AR Post North of McMahon Line due to faulty (or non-existent) maps. Dalvi of 7 Brigade (Towang) nor Amrik of 4 Division (or Niranjan his successor) played NO active part & 'privately' had no faith in the Forward Policy. Merely post-officed things to Delhi. Having discarded original Dhola – Dhola 2 came into being, further North, & resulted in Chinese ire.

On 7/8 Sep 1962, Chinese ex Thagla surrounded Dhola 2, leaving, as usual, one side uncovered - an incentive for defenders escaping or desertion depending upon how you look upon it. This incident resulted in a political furore in Parliament.

Within a month of this happening, IV Corps, under Biji Kaul, was born on the night of 3rd October 1962. A little after midnight of 3/4 October, I was awakened by the DMI (Bim Batra), summoned to Biji's house, and was appointed (superseding some others) CSO IV Corps. (I had never worked with Biji but had known the NEFA Region while in 33 Corps). It was an unappetizing task - there were no resources, no planning. Adhocism was rife – yet a major operation was envisaged under some really un-surmountable difficulties of terrain, altitude, weather, seven days from the road-head.

Biji and I, plus two of his 'favourites' -Lt Cols Pachnanda & Sanjeev Rao- left for Tezpur on 4 Oct 1962 around 10 AM, in the Presidential Viking aircraft. We were received at Tezpur Airport by Bogey Sen, HK Sibal, & Umrao. Confabulations commenced immediately and lasted till 10 PM. It was clear enough that barring Thapar, Sen & Biji none else believed that the Chinese could be engaged in Namka Chu (Dhola 2) region. Also had surfaced, a distinct Sen/Umrao personality clash. Sen had been telling anyone willing to listen 'Dhola could be secured but for Umrao's intransigence'. Sitting in Lucknow how he reached this conclusion remains a mystery.

Umrao's reasoned warnings – he had submitted in September under his own signature two really telling 'Appreciations' of the Situation- were not heeded. He even cautioned Biji (on night of 4$^{th}$ Oct) in my presence, friendly like – *apki bezzati hone wali hai*). Biji went headlong to needle the Chinese - by then Nehru had declared that Kaul had been sent to 'throw out' the Chinese- (privately) believing IB Malik's assurances - Chinese will not go to war!!!!

## Brigadier Tery Baretto – Air Support Signal Unit (ASSU)

ASSU HQ was located in Palam (Delhi Cantt). Its tentacles were spread all over Ladakh. Each tentacle consisted of three men, a WS 62, a 300 W charging engine and a 40 lb. tent.

I visited some of these tentacles when I was CSO Western Command, and was distressed to see the condition of these small detachments attached to infantry battalions. I particularly remember the one at Thoise and their little 40 lb. tent, completely uncared for.

I tried, unsuccessfully, to impress on Signals Directorate and the Air Force that I could not guarantee communication with WS 62 from these tentacles in Ladakh to Palam. These tentacles were designed to call for support from air-fields in North Africa which were within 40 miles of the front.

I had on my office table in Simla the wireless diagram of the ASSU layout. When the Chinese attacked, I read the SITREP every morning.

One by one these infantry battalions were over run and with them the ASSU detachment. I crossed out the relevant circle in my diagram. Eventually there were hardly any left. In any case, as Air Force was not used, air support was never called for.

I tried to plan a control station at Srinagar which would relay calls for air support by SCR-399 to Palam but the Air Force did not agree.

I kept the ASSU wireless diagram with the Corps History files in the leather *yakdan* which I handed over to STC Jabalpur when I retired. If that box has been traced, it may still be there.

## Colonel BS Panwar – Impressions on the Sino – India Conflict in NEFA -1962

Colonel Panwar commanded "Signal Task Force" during 1962-62. The Task Force was at that time employed on construction of permanent line routes in NEFA. Col Panwar was asked to give an account of the line communication systems existing at that period in NEFA so that an idea of the communication systems existing during the Sino-Indian conflict 1962 in NEFA could be understood in the correct perspective.

Col Panwar brought out that he raised two Task Forces at the General Reserve Engineering Forces (GREF) Centre at Allahabad. He ensured that they had the requisite manpower and were fully equipped before they proceeded out of the Centre. One of the Task Forces was raised for project BEACON which was then committed in Jammu and Kashmir. After raising this Task Force, Lt Col SN Atal took it to Jammu and Kashmir.

The second Task Force that he raised was for project TUSKER. The Force was earmarked to proceed to NEFA. He took the Force to NEFA and reached the Foothills at Misamari. Prior to raising this Task Force, he had carried out extensive reconnaissance of the area that the Force was to operate in.

The task Force consisted of three companies. One company comprised jawans from the Corps of Signals. The other two companies comprised personnel from the GREF. The Task Force reached Tezpur on the 51[st] anniversary of the Corps i.e., on 15[th] February 1962. Tezpur, those days was the Headquarters of 4 Infantry Division.

The priority task undertaken by the Force after arriving in NEFA was to construct the following two routes:-

(a) North Lakhimpur – Lakhabali – Along.

(b) Tezpur – Misamari (Foothills) – Dirang Dzong – Bomdila – Tawang.

Both the routes were to be built up on 300 pounds copper wire. To start with only one pair was to be built on each of the two routes. One of the routes had reached just short of Bomdila when in September 1962, the Chinese started infiltrating across the border. Immediately after the infiltration commenced, Col Panwar ensured that only regular army personnel were used for the construction ahead of Bomdila whereas GREF personnel were used for construction work, well to the rear of the border.

Commencement of infiltration could possibly be called as the start of hostilities for no declaration of war was even given. The Task Force was under the command of 4 Division; however, the infiltration by the Chinese was initially not taken very seriously by people at Command and Army Headquarters.

The Task Force helped the movement of troops from Tezpur to Dhola by providing them all the transport which they had. The transport fleet with the Task Force (who then had Nissan vehicles) was certainly better than that with the Division which largely held the Second World War vintage 15 cwt. Trucks. It became clear that the Chinese had infiltrated in all seriousness and meant business. Col Panwar speeded up the construction of the route to Bomdila – Dirang Dzong – Sela – Tawang. A certain amount of disorderliness did prevail and post haste the new 4 Corps Headquarters was formed. Lt Gen BM Kaul went as the Corps Commander whereas Brig PS Gill was the CSO and Brig ID Verna was posted as the Brigadier in Charge Administration.

The next major movement took place on 20th October, 1962. Large scale movement was carried out by the Chinese where they overwhelmed 7 Infantry Brigade. 7 Infantry Brigade suffered very heavy casualties. All their three battalions lost a large amount of personnel who were killed. The balance of the brigade was almost taken as prisoners. Lt Col KK Tewari, who was at that time visiting 1/9 GR was also taken a prisoner. The remnants of the Indian troops quickly withdrew to Sela.

At that time, Col Panwar managed to obtain some radio sets AN/TRC with which he established a radio relay link. The radio relay link was established from Bomdila to Sela to provide duplex speech.

The next major action that took place was on 17 to 20 Nov. Once again, Chinese amassed troops and crossed the border. Col Panwar, at that time, was with his troops seeing a film in the Mess. His Adjutant, Capt SVS Chaudhury quietly walked up to him and told him that both Bomdila and Dirang Dzong were cut off. Col Panwar immediately spoke to the BGS, Brig KK Singh. It was then realized that the Chinese had once again infiltrated and had cut off the lines.

Next day, 18 Nov, Bomdila fell. Col Panwar spoke to Lt Col GS Sodhi, who had taken command of the 4 Infantry Divisional Signal Regiment from Lt Col KK Tewari, who had been captured prisoner. Lt Col Sodhi informed him that they were abandoning Bomdila within the next hour. Six personnel of the Corps who were part of the Task Force and were involved in the maintenance of the lines ahead of Bomdila were killed.

All efforts to hold the Bomdila Fort proved of no avail. The Chinese troops which came in wave after wave were able to capture the fort. Utter Chaos prevailed on the Indian side.

The next day on 19 Nov, 5 Infantry Division was flown in. Lt Col HS Kler was the Commander Signals.

It was found that the Corps Headquarters moved out from Tezpur to Gauhati. Further by evening of 20 Nov, Chinese declared a unilateral cease fire. Later it was discovered that almost the entire route built up by the Task Force had been stripped of the copper wire. The Chinese had possibly taken away all the copper.

## Lieutenant General D N Varma - Some "Experiences" of the Indo China War of 1962

In 1962 as a young lieutenant with about three years' service I was posted at 1 Air Formation Signal Regiment located in Delhi Cantt. As can be imagined I was enjoying life, till one late evening in first week of Oct, I was summoned, told that I had the (un)enviable designation of 'officer on special duty Air Headquarters'. I was told to move forthwith to Gauhati with my Wing Signal Section of 1 JCO, 40 other ranks, a jeep and six trucks loaded with equipment.

The first task was to provide 'landline' communications to the newly raised 20 Wing Air Force located in an old Army barracks near Gauhati Air Field. It was also the forward Headquarters of the AOC-in-C Eastern Air Command, aptly nicknamed AVM 'Tiger Singh'. Needless to say we quickly went about establishing communications - a 40 line F&F local exchange; trunk lines to other Wing HQs, Calcutta & Delhi hired from Department of Telecommunications (DOT) and terminated on a T 43 Trunk Board. I was privy to some fascinating trunk calls from the Defence Minister, but that must wait another day. We also upgraded communications at other air fields in NEFA (North East Frontier Agency) now named Arunachal Pradesh. Youngsters today would be amazed to hear of some of the equipment we operated, many of which are in museums today and should possibly have been at that time too.

Our first taste of war was when on 20$^{th}$ October, China launched their first major offensive against 7 Infantry Brigade. About 40 serious casualties were evacuated via Gauhati to Shillong. They were staged for the night in our make shift medical room which had only one Medical Officer and one nursing assistant. I volunteered to help – uneasy initiation from the theoretical to practical aspects of war.

Hectic activities started. We hardly had time for the basics let alone the niceties of life. One day in middle of it all I was summoned by the DCSO Area who was visiting Gauhati. He had visited the airfield and found that line communications there were 'not properly laid'. As per him, all communications at air field were the responsibility of

Air Formation Signals. In the politest manner that could be mustered up in the middle of the chaos and confusion, I informed him that these were of Rear 4 Infantry Division and looked after by 4 Infantry Divisional Signal Regiment. Not liking my 'cheek' he turned to the officer next to him and said "put him under close arrest". On the other hand 'Tiger Singh' took it as a personal affront that someone had dared touch one of his officers. Only a signal from CAFSO, Air HQ and Brigadier Pettengel, then CSO Eastern Command defused matters and set me free. I was 'rewarded' by promotion to Captain.

Air Force decided to establish a Tactical HQ near Tezpur to better control air operations in conjunction with 4 Corps. I with a few detachments moved to the Tactical HQ and established communications, HQ 4 Corps was also connected. A conference was setup on 20th Nov morning between CSO 4 Corps and Wing Commander, CSO Air Force Tactical HQ. On reaching the Corps HQ we were 'greeted' with a scene of great turbulence. The Corps HQ was packing up to move out of Tezpur. We were tersely told that "We will meet you on the other side of the River". We learnt that Chinese were at the foot hills just a little distance away.

We rushed straight back. The news of the Army's move was met with great deal of incredulity and annoyance. 4 Corps had not found it fit to give any advance notice to the Air Force. The Mess, Canteen and other administrative establishments wore a deserted look as all civilian staff had fled. There was no food to be had. Of course, canteen doors had been flung open and there was plenty of beer and some tinned food available. All officers were issued a pistol and three rounds and airmen, a rifle and 10 rounds. We were ready to face the Chinese Army.

During all this confusion it was decided to wire up the bomb dump to 'blow up' if and when the Chinese turned up. I was tasked to lay a line from the Ops Room to the Bomb Dump, a distance of about 12 km. It was planned to install a Morse key at the Ops room which when pressed would blow up the Bomb dump. I at my 'technical best' decided not to trust the insulation of D3 field cable whose short would have caused the Bomb dump to blow up and cause major destruction.

So we laid two pairs, one on either side of the road! Fortunately the eventuality did not arise.

Shortly thereafter, plans were made to evacuate Tezpur. Available transport aircraft were flown to Tezpur to load whatever we could. Civilian Tea Garden *wallahs*, mostly "Gora Sahibs" drove up in their big cars and were evacuated to Gauhati. They left the keys of their cars with us with a request to safeguard them. I still recall the big thank you party they gave on 30th Nov, when they came back after things had returned to normal. Incidentally, no Army person was given an airlift. So much for Army Air Force relations!

On 24th Nov, a Top Secret Flash message was received from Air HQ. The problem was how to decode it. All cipher documents were supposed to have been destroyed. Quietly, Flt Lt Gaur, last officer on Cipher duty produced OTP documents from under his jacket and sat down on the tarmac to decipher the message, with all of us standing in a ring around him. Tension was palpable. I remember a sheet being blown away by the wind; it was chased by none other than the Station Commander himself, and brought back to Gaur. The message when decoded was simple but terse "Unilateral Ceasefire by China; however, no complacency." Needless to say we all adjourned to the Mess to celebrate end of war in true "Fauji" style.

Since the Tac HQ had moved out to Bagdogra, the Wing Signal Section was also asked to move there. The convoy of seven vehicles moved by road after filling up petrol in all vehicles. A 200 litre barrel was also filled up with petrol. About 100 km from Bagdogra, petrol ran out causing a big problem as there was no Petrol Depot near about. The Section Havildar suggested a simple plan. He and I drove up in a jeep to a roadside petrol pump and got petrol filled up. Then to the surprise of the petrol pump staff, other vehicles pulled up one by one. They were hard put to object. The bill came to about Rs. 385, which was a princely sum in those days. The petrol was one Rupee ten annas a gallon! A signed chit was given to the Petrol Pump owner who had turned up by then citing operational necessity. Regiment's address at Delhi was also give in case... After a couple of months the Regiment received a letter of thanks from the petrol pump owner to say that he had got the money from Gauhati Petrol Depot ASC.

Soon after reaching Bagdogra news was received to move back to Tezpur and re-establish communications. By end of December the Tac HQ moved to Shillong and was upgraded as HQ Eastern Air Command. Wing Signal Section moved back to Delhi and joined the Regiment.

The importance of landline communications was amply brought out after the operations. 3 Air Formation Signal Regiment was raised post haste at Delhi. In May 1963 it moved to Borjhar, Gauhati. I was posted as SO2 Air Formation Signals at the Shillong based Eastern Command and served there till I moved for Degree Engineering Course.

## Major General K.K Tewari - Additional Inputs on 17 May 2009

The role played by the late Lt Gen B. M Kaul (Biji) who was earlier the GOC of this Division and had now become the QMG, was literally to impose his popular ideas of construction of accommodation for troops in Ambala area where the Division was located. Even after the Division was moved to the North Eastern borders for its new defence roles in a mountainous area, vital aspects for study and training for the new role by the troops - for which he would have known that it had no previous experience or training or even equipment, were ignored. The project of building accommodation for troops was given overriding priority by the military and the political hierarchy, first in the peace time location in Punjab as Op AMAR and then in NEFA again as Op AMAR 2. There was a complete neglect of the needs of getting the troops acclimatized to the mountainous areas facing totally different problems. Added to all this was the vast area of operational responsibilities given to the Division and little time allowed to acclimatize the troops and train for war in totally different terrain and problems of support. There were challenges of Op AMAR 2 to compete accommodation within a time frame. This was especially for Signals a unique challenge as the Prime Minister was to inaugurate the AMAR 2 project in the Signal Regimental lines in Tezpur. All this was at the cost of preparedness for war in a totally new type of terrain with special problems for Signals with its available equipment, its suitability or inadequacy and training in usage. I have talked about these things in my book "A Soldier's Voyage of Self Discovery" on Pages 60 to 62.

All this has also to be viewed in context of the flamboyant kind of personalities of the Army hierarchy at the time after the sad departure from the top of popular commanders like Generals Thimayya and Thorat and the imposition of controls and dictation by civilian bureaucrats and other favoured authorities – starting from the Honourable Minister of Defence and his favourites among the Army brass and para- military authorities.

The deployment initially of Assam Rifles as part of Op ONKAR before the launch of Op LEGHORN and the complete confusion on the correct alignment of the border (inclusive or exclusive of Thagle Ridge) at the political level in Delhi and the Army's Command and Corps levels were added factors.

The overall responsibility for coordination of the border defence lay with the Army. That meant that Commander Signals 4 Division had to coordinate all the communication requirements including those with para military forces. For the Divisional Signals, the worst problem faced was the confusion in orders and counter orders from the Tactical HQs of Command, Corps (XXXIII first and then IV Corps) and the Divisional Commander and their staff officers - all present in Tezpur together at the same time frequently. Added to this was the tendency of certain senior personalities to score points and blame the inadequacy of communications. What the Signals had to do was to perform miracles with outdated equipment, its shortages, lack of repair facilities and its transportation to forward areas man/ mule pack basis. I have mentioned all this on Pages 71 to 74 of my book in detail.

It needs to be emphasized how we were able to buy and put to use some radio and other communication equipment auctioned in 1946 at the end of World War 2 and lying with some shopkeepers in North

East at places like Tinsukhia (mention made of this on Page 64 of my book). All this needs to be brought out for posterity.

In the Preview on Pages 1 and 2 of your draft, it would be good to mention about the Chinese betrayal of the Panchsheel Agreement of 1954. Also an earlier report by Lt Gen Kalwant Singh on the defence of our Northern borders, after the Longju incident in August 1959 (when the Assam Rifles post was overcome by the Chinese) and a similar one in Ladakh, was completely ignored. All this was due to the "political" enthusiasm at the time of the popular "Hindi Chini Bhai Bhai" slogan. This was also about the time when Gen Thimayya had and Lt Gen Thorat also had left and the Minister of Defence had his selected "mouldable" military brass to head the Army. It was to have a major impact on the control and functioning of the armed forces in the following years with the resultant consequences in effective defence of the borders. There was also the flawed intelligence about the Chinese and neglect of the physical preparedness of the army for high mountainous defences and its equipment/ weapons.

In the Conclusion, it would be good to emphasise a few special points for Signals History aspect. I quote a few examples from the latest literature you have sent me, as recorded in my reminiscences to show how ill prepared the Army was in 1962. The extraordinary demands on 4 Divisional Signal Regiment personnel of not just providing communication cover for its Division but a Corps HQ imposed on it (before its own Corps Signal Regiment could be created) and earlier with Tactical HQ of Command and Corps (XXXIII) and IGAR in Tezpur at the same time. On top of it was the exceptional demands of direct communications addressed not just to the next higher or lower formations but direct to Command HQ and Delhi with Flash and Top Secret classifications. To add to all this unusual and load were the numerous para military forces like SIB, AR, Tusker (Border roads) with their needs/ demands. All this has to be viewed from a psychological angle of those days when our Intelligence said that only one in three Chinese is armed and that too with old Japanese rifles with defective ammunition. We were also told all too often not to complain and flap as the Chinese are not going to attack, quoting the highest authority in the defence set up – Minister level.

Besides the various difficulties listed above, the most vital and difficult problem faced by Signals was by the personalities of the senior commanders. Just to quote one example for record. For a three star general to give a 2/3 page message at a forward post on 5 Oct (even before the troops had time to settle down and establish communications on obsolete radio equipment which had been man packed up there) not only marked as FLASH and TOPSECRET but addressed to the highest in Delhi political authorities with copies to intermediate Army formations like Command and Corps HQ – just shows complete disregard and even basic knowledge of available communication facilities in the new field area. There were no machine cipher facilities for enciphering but only the book ciphers of low classification and Morse code key transmission of enciphered version. Number of available cipher staff was another major factor – only meant to cater for normal divisional traffic and not be flooded with traffic imposed big higher commanders. Should not the worthy Corps Commander have known this? All this was to be at the expense of establishing minimum communication channels and coping with their primary responsibilities of handling Signals traffic at brigade, divisional level for normal functioning while still in the process of settling down.

Literally, it was an impossible situation and it is being described by one who was involved personally as the Commander Signals of the Division at the time - by one, who had gone through Burma operations in World War 2 with air supply and other facilities. And now in Oct 1962, to be faced with denial of even basic clothing and equipment and on top of that to be imposed with impossible demands while being threatened with consequences, in case of failure.

Saddest part of the 1962 war is the fact that even though an official enquiry was held about it by a senior serving officer – Lt Gen Henderson Brooks - this report has not been made public to this date more than 45 years later. The obvious implication would be to protect the role played by certain personalities in the political field or military hierarchy at the time.

I think, what I have given above and earlier on 12 Mar 09 is the best I can give you and you have the liberty to take what you want as the author of the Corps History.

All my good wishes and best of luck for the wonderful work you have under taken. God bless.

Krishna Tewari

# BIBLIOGRAPHY

Cardozo, Maj. Gen. Ian (ed.), *The Indian Army - A Brief History*, New Delhi, United Service Institution of India, 2005.

Dalvi, Brigadier J.P., *Himalayan Blunder,* Thacker and Company, Bombay, 1969,

Johri, Major Sita Ram, *Chinese Invasion of NEFA*, Himalaya Publications, Lucknow,

Kaul, Lieutenant General B.M. *The Untold Story,* Allied Publishers, New Delhi, 1967

Maxwell, Neville, *India's China War,* Cape, London, 1970

Menezes, Lt. Gen. S.L., *Fidelity and Honour – The Indian Army from the Seventeenth to the Twenty First Century*, Penguin, New Delhi, 1993.

Mullik, B.N. *The Chinese Betrayal,* Allied Publishers, New Delhi.

Palit, Major General D.K., *War in High Himalaya – The Indian Army in Crisis, 1962,* Natraj Publishers, Dehradun, 1969

Prasad, Major General Niranjan, *The Fall of Towang, 1962,* Palit & Palit, New Delhi,

Praval, K.C., *Indian Army After Independence*, New Delhi, Lancer Publishers, 2009.

Singh, Brigadier Lakshman, *Letters from the Border and Other Less Told Stories,* B.L.S Publishers, NOIDA, 2003

Singh, Maj. Gen. V.K., *Leadership in the Indian Army – Biographies of Twelve Soldiers,* Sage Publications, New Delhi, 2005

Tewari, Major General K.K., *A Soldier's Voyage of Self Discovery,* Auroville, 1995.

Thorat, Lt. Gen. S.P.P., *From Reveille to Retreat,* New Delhi, Allied Publishers, 1986.

www.ingramcontent.com/pod-product-compliance
Ingram Content Group UK Ltd.
Pitfield, Milton Keynes, MK11 3LW, UK
UKHW041824200726
13854UKWH00002BA/539